GOSPEL FOUNDATIONS®

Longing for a King

VOL. 3 | 1 SAMUEL – 1 KINGS

LifeWay Press® • Nashville, Tennessee

From the creators of *The Gospel Project*, Gospel Foundations® is a six-volume resource that teaches the storyline of Scripture. It is comprehensive in scope yet concise enough to be completed in just one year. Each seven-session volume includes videos to help your group understand the way each text fits into the storyline of the Bible.

© 2018 LifeWay Press® • Reprinted April 2019

ISBN 978-1-5359-0360-8 • Item 005803634

Dewey decimal classification: 230
Subject headings: CHRISTIANITY / GOSPEL / SALVATION

EDITORIAL TEAM

Michael Kelley
Director, Discipleship and Groups Ministry

Brian Dembowczyk
Managing Editor

Joel Polk
Editorial Team Leader

Daniel Davis, Josh Hayes
Content Editors

Brian Daniel
Manager, Short-Term Discipleship

Darin Clark
Art Director

We believe that the Bible has God for its author; salvation for its end; and truth, without any mixture of error, for its matter and that all Scripture is totally true and trustworthy. To review LifeWay's doctrinal guideline, please visit lifeway.com/doctrinalguideline.

Scripture quotations are taken from the Christian Standard Bible®, Copyright © 2017 by Holman Bible Publishers. Used by permission. Christian Standard Bible® and CSB® are federally registered trademarks of Holman Bible Publishers.

To order additional copies of this resource, write to LifeWay Resources Customer Service; One LifeWay Plaza; Nashville, TN 37234; fax 615-251-5933; call toll free 800-458-2772; order online at LifeWay.com; email orderentry@lifeway.com; or visit the LifeWay Christian Store serving you.

Printed in the United States of America

Groups Ministry Publishing • LifeWay Resources
One LifeWay Plaza • Nashville, TN 37234

Contents

About *The Gospel Project*

Gospel Foundations is from the creators of *The Gospel Project*, which exists to point kids, students, and adults to the gospel of Jesus Christ through weekly group Bible studies and additional resources that show how God's plan of redemption unfolds throughout Scripture and still today, compelling them to join the mission of God.

The Gospel Project provides theological yet practical, age-appropriate Bible studies that immerse your entire church in the story of the gospel, helping to develop a gospel culture that leads to gospel mission.

Gospel Story

Immersing people of all ages in the storyline of Scripture: God's plan to rescue and redeem His creation through His Son, Jesus Christ.

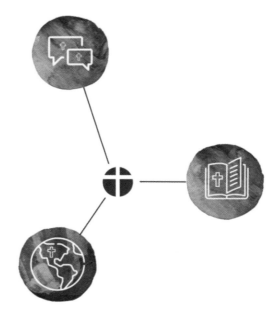

Gospel Culture

Inspiring communities where the gospel saturates our experience and doubters become believers who become declarers of the gospel.

Gospel Mission

Empowering believers to live on mission, declaring the good news of the gospel in word and deed.

How to Use This Study

This Bible-study book includes seven weeks of content for group and personal study.

Group Study

Regardless of what day of the week your group meets, each week of content begins with the group session. Each group session uses the following format to facilitate simple yet meaningful interaction among group members and with God's Word.

Introducing the Study & Setting the Context
These pages include **content and questions** to get the conversation started and **infographics** to help group members see the flow of the biblical storyline.

Continuing the Discussion
Each session has a corresponding **teaching video** to help tell the Bible story. These videos have been created specifically to challenge the group to consider the entire story of the Bible. After watching the video, continue the **group discussion** by reading the Scripture passages and discussing the questions on these pages. Finally, conclude each group session with **a personal missional response** based on what God has said through His Word.

Personal Study

Three personal studies are provided for each session to take individuals deeper into Scripture and to supplement the content introduced in the group study. With **biblical teaching and introspective questions**, these sections challenge individuals to grow in their understanding of God's Word and to respond in faith.

Leader Guide

A tear-out leader guide for each session is provided on pages 95-108, which includes possible answers to questions highlighted with an icon and suggestions for various sections of the group study.

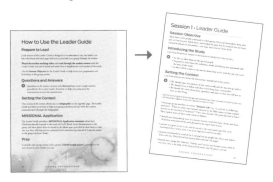

God's Word to You

We Need the True King

The last verse in the Book of Judges—a book that chronicles the downward spiral of disobedience of those who were called to be radically different as the people of God— is one of the most depressing verses in the Bible: "In those days there was no king in Israel; everyone did whatever seemed right to him" (Judg. 21:25).

Is this not a fitting definition of sin? In this one verse, we see the prideful root of self-lordship, self-exaltation, and self-determination at the core of all our rebellion. We are, in our own minds, the gods of our own universe. And as such, we have the right to choose whatever is right and wrong for ourselves, and anything that imposes some authority over us other than our own autonomous minds, hearts, and desires is a constraint that must be thrown off.

As sinners, we are like the Israelites of old, convinced of our own truth, our own ideas, and our own wisdom. Our sin has blinded us to what is truly good and right, and it's precisely because of this blindness that we need a true king.

We need a king who tells us the truth, guides us with justice, and leads us in righteousness. And we need a king who can open our eyes to all these things and more. But because we are enslaved by our own desires, the true king we need must not only be our ruler but also our rescuer.

In Jesus, we find this King—the One before whom every knee will bow and whose greatness every tongue will eventually confess.

In Jesus, the true King has come. He is the King of love as well as the King of power.

In Jesus, and in Him alone, will we finally find all our desires for peace, security, and wholeness met.

What is left for us, then, is to acknowledge that every other king we seek to enthrone is only a substitute for Jesus. Far better is for us to trust in Him not only as our rescuer but also as our ruler and to acknowledge that all authority that has been given to Him.

God's People Demand a King

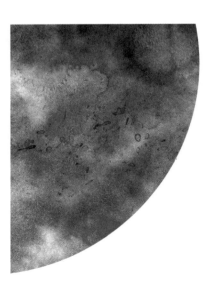

Introducing the Study

God made good on His word. Despite the spiritual wandering of His people, He delivered them into a land of their own. But the blessing of the promised land came with renewed warnings for God's people. God wanted His people set apart, both in belief and in lifestyle, loving and trusting His rule and following Him only. This new land, though, brought great temptation for the people of God to compromise.

✳ Why does God desire His people to be set apart from the world?

I'm not sure. but what I think is he wants those set apart because believers act on faith. vs what can be seen & heard. believers of God are examples to those around.

God had always been faithful to His people. He provided for them, loved them, and rescued them over and over again. He proved Himself to be both good and great, loving and powerful. These are the marks of what we long for in a true king. But the question for God's people, both then and now, is where we can find a true king? The answer is only in Jesus, who now rules and reigns over all.

Where do you see the longing for a true king in our culture today?

Hmm. well, many people are lost, lonely & guideless. this includes me. lots of fear happening in the world and also the human separation & people's pride/ego/self-absorbance, etc. getting in the way of a healthy community. our world lacks connection of what really matters.

Setting the Context

The Book of Judges closes with one of the saddest verses in the entire Bible: "In those days there was no king in Israel; everyone did whatever seemed right to him" (Judges 21:25). Having settled into the land, the people also settled into a state of **spiritual anarchy**, with each person determining their own truth and their own path. During those days, the high priest, **Eli**, seemingly representative of the people, failed to provide anything close to the spiritual and moral leadership the Lord demanded.

> How are the temptations the people faced in the promised land similar to the temptations Christians face in our culture today?
>
> *Very similar. Many of us follow blindly because we are seeking guidance, community & a sense of belonging even if its not right.*

Yet there were some who were faithful to the Lord. **Hannah**, for example, was a devout woman who prayed and asked the Lord to give her a son, though she was unable to conceive. The Lord answered her prayer, and she named her son **Samuel** and dedicated him to the Lord and His service. The Lord began to speak to Samuel, even while he was very young, and fulfilled everything that Samuel prophesied. Samuel delivered God's word and judged the people, and there was a period of relative peace in the land. **"Samuel's Life"** (p. 11) provides an overview of this man's ministry in Israel.

Still, the people were not satisfied. And as Samuel grew older, a stirring arose in Israel to reject God alone as their King.

> ✳ What ought to be our response when we recognize that Jesus is the King we really need?
>
> *Well, for me, I think its on the person and everyones experience w/ God is different. I think a certain experience or few can make it or break it for someone. I think others can tell you things & persuade you to believe in God, but ultimately, I believe we each have a unique journey w/ God that can only be alone. Whether we choose to believe/follow is up to the person & is btwn them/God. Gods timing is everything.*

✚ CHRIST Connection

The people of Israel rejected God as their King and demanded a human king to be like the nations around them despite God's warnings. God gave His people Saul, who failed to trust and obey God, which brought his reign to an end. Israel needed a king who would trust and obey God fully to establish a lasting kingdom. Jesus is that King, and through His perfect obedience, God would establish His rule over His people forever.

Samuel's *Life*

YOUNG MAN

- Miraculously born to Hannah and Elkanah (1 Sam. 1:20)
- Weaned and given to the Lord, as Hannah had promised (1:23-28)
- Heard the word of the Lord for the first time (3:1-14)

JUDGE

- Officiated over a covenant renewal for the people (7:2-6)
- Judged Israel throughout his life (7:15)

THE KING-MAKER

- Grew old and appointed his sons as judges, but they were wicked (8:1-3)
- Heard the Israelites' demand for a king and gave God's response (8:4-22)

SAUL
- Anointed Saul as ruler over Israel (10:1)
- Arrived to offer a sacrifice, but Saul had already offered it (13:10-12)
- Gave command to destroy the Amalekites, but Saul disobeyed (15:1-9)
- Killed King Agag of Amalek as Saul should have done (15:32-33)

DAVID
- Anointed David as king over Israel (16:1-13)
- Died and was mourned by all Israel (25:1)
- Called up as a spirit by Saul through a medium (28:11-19)

Continuing the Discussion

▶ Watch this session's video, and then continue the group discussion using the following guide.

Why do you think we struggle with the idea of having a king?
Fear of judgement, losing control over our lives.

What, in your opinion, would the ideal king be like?
A balance. He is an honest, yet kind King.

As a group, read 1 Samuel 8:4-9,19-20.

What did the people ask Samuel to do, and what was so wicked about this request?

Does their request make sense to you? Why or why not?

✱ In what ways might we reject God as King?

Samuel was getting older and his sons were not fit to take his place. The people longed for stable and trustworthy leadership, and so, they asked for an earthly king. While this request may seem harmless, it reveals that the people were rejecting the reason God had intentionally not given them an earthly king—He was to be their king. This was one of the ways they were to be different from the world. God, however, would grant their request, and give them Saul as their first king.

As a group, read 1 Samuel 13:6-9,13-14.

What can you learn about Saul based on these verses?

What would be different about the next king God would provide for Israel?

✱ Based on these verses, what are the things that are important to God?

Saul certainly looked the part of a king, but in his heart, he was never committed to God's rule over him. Instead of following the law of God, Saul took matters into his own hands, trusting in himself, and as a result, God rejected him. Even still, God promised that He would raise up another king who would be a man after His own heart.

As a group, read 1 Samuel 15:10-11,22-23.

What would you say God desires from His people?

In what ways might you be like Saul?

✳ How should we, if God is our King, treat the Word of God?

Saul might have had some examples of external obedience, but his heart was far from God. This is what God is truly after—not merely occasional obedience but a heart that loves Him and His rule. The only way we can truly please God, then, is when our hearts have been changed by the gospel. When that happens, we joyously accept God's rule and reign over our lives and pray for His kingdom to come.

✝ MISSIONAL Application

Record in this space at least one way you will apply the truth of Scripture as a humble servant of the King of kings.

Personal Study 1

The people reject God as their true King.

Read 1 Samuel 8:4-9,19-20.

Samuel was the boy who was miraculously born to Hannah and then grew up to be one of Israel's greatest prophets. He heard directly from God and then spoke on behalf of God to the people. However, Samuel's sons turned from the Lord, and their rebellion provided the chance for Israel to request something they had been itching for—a king like all the nations around them had.

The people's request seemed innocent and even logical. They longed for security and stability. Yet Samuel sensed that the people's request represented a lack of trust in God. God was supposed to be their true King, since they were to depend on Him for everything. But the people were asking for something *other than* God to bring them security. They wanted to place their trust in an earthly king instead.

Surely we can relate. Is it not easier to "trust God" when everything that you think you need for life is right in front of you? Your job is secure, your marriage is fulfilling, and everyone you care about is healthy. But when one of these things is missing, do you notice a feeling of insecurity or anxiety or unhappiness arising within you?

This is where Israel was. They wanted a king they could see and touch and control. And God saw their request as a rejection because everything about His character proved that they could trust Him.

God called their request for a king disobedience, but then He acquiesced. If this request was so bad, why did God give it to them? Why not simply say no? This is why: God will sometimes answer your prayers to let you learn the hard way that your motivation was wrong. In other words, God's judgment here was to answer all of their desires with a yes: "For this reason God delivered them over to disgraceful passions" (Rom. 1:26).

Even though Israel had been warned that a human king would ultimately abuse his power, they still demanded one. They wanted someone they could see who would "fight their battles." They were forfeiting the very thing that set them apart from every other nation and that had brought victory time and time again.

Similarly, when people who have been redeemed by Christ look to things in this world for protection, security, and validation, they start to look like everyone else. Forgetting their identity and the love that comes from a restored relationship with God, they become bound to a "king" they think will satisfy them. This pursuit leads to the obsessive, overworking, and destructive behavior that we have discussed previously. With this type of behavior, it is difficult to distinguish between professing Christians and the rest of the world.

This is not what God intended for His people. This is not what He intends for you. He wants you to know the love and assurance that comes from knowing Christ.

What are some things that make you feel secure?

What are the signs that we are trusting in these things for our security and not in God alone?

In what ways do we stand out from the world when we trust in God alone as King?

Personal Study 2

The people's king fails to trust God.

Read 1 Samuel 13:6-9,13-14.

God gave the people what they wanted. Saul, who was thirty years old when he became king, looked the part. He reigned for forty-two years and did exactly what God promised an earthly king would do: he conscripted an army and appointed them to fight for Israel.

God gave Saul some military successes, but as his reign over Israel continued, he found himself facing an equally powerful Philistine army. What's worse, the Israelites were not positioned for victory in battle. Saul and his troops were growing restless; many in the army were moving well beyond anxiety into fear. But still they waited at Gilgal for Samuel the prophet to come and give them a word from the Lord.

Samuel would come, they hoped, and offer a sacrifice to the Lord and tell them what to do. The army knew that if the Lord was on their side, then He would deliver the Philistines into their hands, so they waited for Samuel to come and bring confirmation. They waited for seven days, and still Samuel did not come.

Have you ever felt that way? That there was some great task in front of you, one that you were incapable of completing without the Lord's help? And yet, no matter how much you prayed, it felt like God was silent? What do we typically do when that happens? Most of the time, we do exactly what Saul did—we take matters into our own hands.

Abraham knew that God had promised to make him into a great nation, but years passed without a child, and so, he took matters into his own hands. He conceived a child not with Sarah but with her servant Hagar. Moses knew that it was wrong for the Israelites, God's people, to be enslaved to the Egyptians, so rather than waiting on God's method and timing, he took matters into his own hands and murdered an Egyptian. Later, in the New Testament, Peter believed Jesus was the Messiah, but instead of waiting on God's fulfillment of Jesus' identity, Peter took matters into his own hands and attacked a soldier with a sword.

Saul knew there was a prescribed manner for sacrifices to be offered. He knew this was specifically something for the priest to do, and yet in his impatience, he took it upon himself. He offered the sacrifices. Like Abraham, like Moses, and like Peter, Saul demonstrated his lack of trust in God by presuming that he could manufacture victory, safety, and security on his own.

The tale of Saul is a cautionary one for us, for we are people who find it difficult to wait and trust. And yet, this is what God has required of us (Heb. 11:6). We might have the right idea; we might even have the right aspiration or goal. But if we try to proceed forward on our own, we reveal that our trust is not really in God; it's in our own ability to manufacture an end result.

Contrary to the example of this king who did not trust, we find Jesus, the King who did. For in His hour of dire need, Jesus did not presume upon the will of God or take matters into His own hands. Rather, He bent His knee to the plan and purpose of the Father, praying, "Not my will, but yours, be done" (Luke 22:42). Jesus is the King who trusts, and therefore, Jesus is the King who was obedient even to death on a cross.

What is one situation in your life right now in which you are tempted to take matters into your own hands?

What are some warning signs for you to know if you have moved from a posture of trust?

Personal Study 3

The people's king fails to obey God.

Read 1 Samuel 15:10-11,22-23.

First Samuel 15 opens with God giving a clear command to King Saul to conquer the Amalekites and not spare anyone or anything—not even the animals. This was to fulfill God's word to Moses and Joshua that the Amalekites would be destroyed for their attack on the Israelites in the wilderness after they left Egypt—for they did not "fear God" (Ex. 17:14; Deut. 25:17-19). But Saul refused to follow God's instructions completely. He did conquer the Amalekites, but he did not follow through with everything God told him to do. So God spoke to the prophet Samuel, making it clear that Saul's disobedience would have consequences.

The language is very striking as the Lord said, "I regret…" This seems like a strange emotion to attribute to God, doesn't it? The Hebrew word is sometimes even translated "repent." What does it mean for God to regret a past decision, or even worse, to repent of something He has done?

When God uses language like "I regret," He is speaking in terms we can understand. This phrase means that He truly holds regard for the pain of our current circumstances, not that He is unaware of the future. The word *regret* refers to God's necessary distaste for human sin and its effects, and it differs from the way humans experience this emotion (see Num. 23:19; 1 Sam. 15:29). God shows compassion for our sake when our decisions are harmful, but He does not share the pervasive human sentiment of wishing He could just go back and fix a past mistake.

God delivered the unsavory news about Saul's disobedience to Samuel, who was rightfully angry. It moved him to cry and pray all night long and to go to Saul at the first chance he had, early the next morning.

When Samuel arrived, Saul was throwing his victory party. Before he even arrived, word had come to Samuel that Saul had set up a monument elsewhere—*to himself*—in honor of his recent victory. Not only had Saul disregarded the clear command of God, but he also was in the midst of recasting the entire battle to make it about himself.

When Saul greeted Samuel, he boasted of his obedience. Take a moment and consider the craziness of this scene. The evidence of his disobedience was *literally* all around him: sheep making noises and the air filled with the smell of livestock. Yet he carried himself with the air of approval. "That's right," he said proudly, "I am faithfully following the Lord."

We shouldn't simply look at Saul and shake our heads. This story doesn't let us off the hook. How many of us show up at worship services each week acting as if everything is just fine between God and us? How many of us sing songs and put on a good show? Meanwhile, the evidence of our disobedience is all around us. Our spouses, our children, our roommates or coworkers—they know our hypocrisy. They see our halfhearted obedience as the disobedience it truly is.

God is not pleased by people simply singing some songs and giving some of their money. What thrills God is a heart that obeys Him. In other words, what thrills God is a surrendered heart that rests in His grace, not in empty obedience rooted in a desire for human approval. Because we have trusted in Christ, we can actually repent with confidence. We can readily confess our sin and turn to God, without equivocation, knowing that His grace is more than great enough to receive us.

Why do you think we are so prone to partial obedience instead of complete obedience to God's commands?

How can we tell the difference between true repentance over sin and mere regret over sin's consequences?

God Chooses a New King

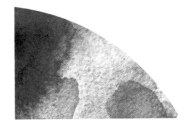

Introducing the Study

Israel's first king certainly looked the part. He was, by human standards, the ideal candidate. Yet his reign was marked by trust in himself rather than in God, and so, the Lord took the kingdom away from him. The people were mistaken in thinking that they could find security and safety through an earthly ruler.

> **How might we make the same mistake of looking for security in people and places rather than in God?**

God does not operate by the standards of humanity. Whereas human beings might focus on appearance, God looks deeply into the heart. When God was ready to anoint the next king of Israel, He would not do so based on popular opinion or outward appearance. Instead, God would give His people one whose heart was bent toward Him.

 Why is it both encouraging and discouraging to know that God looks past outward appearances?

Setting the Context

Saul was the king that had every advantage. He was tall, strong, handsome, and charismatic. By all human standards, he was the ideal candidate for a king. But despite his appearance, Saul demonstrated time and time again during his reign that his heart was far from God. He trusted in himself rather than in God, and God stripped the kingdom from his rule.

> What are some of the effects of rejecting God's loving authority that you have seen?

Once again, **Samuel delivered the word of the Lord**, this time informing Saul of God's decision to take the kingdom from him. Having delivered the news, Samuel and Saul parted ways never to see one another again (at least physically). But the Lord had another message to deliver through His prophet.

Though Saul had failed, **God had chosen his successor**. This time, the king God was choosing would not measure up to the appearance of Saul. In fact, he would be an unlikely choice in every sense of the word. But God would demonstrate through this new king that He looks well beyond external appearance deep into the heart.

This new king, though unexpected, would demonstrate not the power of physical strength, as Saul tried to do, but the power of faith in a mighty God, and this king foreshadowed **"The King of Kings"** (p. 23).

 How should the fact that God looks at the heart change the way we view other people?

✝ CHRIST Connection

In David, we see a picture of an unexpected warrior and king. David defeated a seemingly unbeatable enemy with courageous faith in God's power. Jesus is the greater King whom no one expected to win the victory over sin and death, but through His death and resurrection, He is mighty to save.

The *King of* Kings

Saul

- Of the tribe of Benjamin
- A head taller than anyone else (1 Sam. 9:2)
- Reigned for 42 years

GOOD
- The Spirit of God came on Saul (1 Sam. 10:9-10)
- Credited the Lord with a victory (11:13)
- Fought bravely and defeated the enemies of Israel (14:47-48)

EVIL
- Foolishly offered the burnt offering instead of waiting for Samuel (1 Sam. 13:3-15)
- Disobeyed the command to completely destroy the Amalekites (15:7-31)
- Jealous of David and tried to kill him (18:8-11; 19:9-10; 24:1-22; 26:1-25)
- Consulted a medium to seek guidance for a battle with the Philistines (28:1-25)

David

- Of the tribe of Judah
- A man after God's own heart (1 Sam. 13:14; 16:7)
- Reigned for 40 years

GOOD
- The Spirit of the Lord came on David (1 Sam. 16:13)
- Killed Goliath for the glory of the Lord (17:45-51)
- Spared Saul twice because he was the Lord's anointed, entrusting himself to the Lord's plan (24:1-22; 26:1-25)
- Desired to build a temple for God (2 Sam. 7:1-2; 1 Kings 8:18)

EVIL
- Adultery with Bathsheba and the murder of her husband (2 Sam. 11:1-27)
- Ordered a census of his fighting men (24:1-10)

Jesus

- Son of David, Son of Abraham (Matt. 1:1)
- No form, majesty, or beauty that we should desire Him (Isa. 53:2)
- The Son of David and yet also David's Lord (Matt. 22:41-45)
- His kingdom has no end (Luke 1:33)

GOOD
- There is no sin in Him (Heb. 4:15; 1 John 3:5)
- Jesus is the true Son of God, the delight of His Father (Matt. 3:17)
- Perfectly obeyed the Father, even unto death on a cross to save sinners (Phil. 2:8)
- Had compassion for people, healing the sick and preaching the good news of the kingdom (Matt. 9:35-36)
- Laid down His life for His sheep as the true shepherd (John 10:11-18)
- Resurrected from the dead as the true temple (John 2:19-22)
- He is the King of kings and the Lord of lords (Rev. 19:16)

Continuing the Discussion

▶ Watch this session's video, and then continue the group discussion using the following guide.

What are some reasons it is important for us to remember that God looks at the heart rather than outward appearance?

What are some ways the story of David reminds us of Jesus?

As a group, read 1 Samuel 16:1,6-13.

✳ In what ways does the choice of David defy human standards?

What is a situation in which you've seen God work in surprising ways?

Why might God work in this way? What does doing so tell us about His character?

David, by human standards, was anything but a king. The youngest in his family and not physically imposing, he was an unlikely choice. But God makes unlikely choices like these to demonstrate that He is not bound by human standards and reasoning. Furthermore, God uses unlikely people so that He Himself receives the glory He is due.

As a group, read 1 Samuel 17:23-26,34-37.

✳ How did David demonstrate his faith in these verses?

What can we learn from David's faith?

Why is it important to remember God's faithfulness in the past?

David faced an impossible foe. On his own, he was no match for Goliath. But unlike the rest of the army, David saw the giant as a challenge not to him but to God. He was confident not in his own ability but in God's power, for he had seen God exercise His power in the past. David backed up his claims with action, which showed the validity of his faith.

As a group, read 1 Samuel 17:45-51.

> What is the most striking part to you of David's response to Goliath? Why?

✳ In what ways does David's victory over Goliath foreshadow Jesus' greater victory at the cross and the resurrection?

God's chosen king won an improbable victory for the Lord and His people. God's people, though they did not fight, were delivered through the victory of another. In the same way, we as God's people have been delivered from the greater enemies of sin and death thanks to the victory won on our behalf by Jesus through the cross and resurrection.

✝ MISSIONAL Application

Record in this space at least one way you will apply the truth of Scripture as a herald of the good news that Jesus has defeated the enemies of sin and death.

Personal Study 1

God's king is measured by the Lord's standard, not the world's.

Read 1 Samuel 16:1,6-13.

The prophet Samuel was in deep distress because of Saul's sin. After all, Samuel had anointed him, and Saul had seemed like such a promising prospect. But the king turned out to be nothing like what Samuel or the people had hoped for. Saul was faithful only to himself, and the king's sin grieved the prophet.

God sent Samuel on a mission to find the next king of Israel. Not surprisingly, Samuel was more than a little reluctant to go out to anoint a new king, knowing how passionate the *current* king was about his own kingdom and name and honor. God's plan sounded like a recipe for disaster.

But Samuel ordered a consecration for the sacrifice, in which each member of the community offered themselves to God. This was the perfect moment for Samuel to inspect the sons of Jesse, who would come marching by him in succession.

Eliab was the oldest of Jesse's sons, so he came forward first, looking as kingly as possible. Samuel took one look at him and thought he had found his man—no doubt he was good-looking, tall, and strong. *This* must be kingly material. God, however, was unimpressed. Eliab's appearance, height, and stature did not even register as relevant qualities. God never looks from heaven to judge us by human standards. His criteria are different than what most of us value because He looks into the heart.

In one sense, this is good news. Most of us have tried to measure up to the world's standards, but few people ever feel as if they have been successful. The stress of trying to have the perfect body, a successful career, a conflict-free family—all of these have eluded us. It is refreshing, freeing news that God is not particularly concerned with our earthly successes.

In another sense, though, this is problematic. Who among us has the kind of heart that God would want? Our outward appearance may not be top-notch, but if we are honest with ourselves, our heart condition is rarely much better—and often much worse.

We are not given specific reasons why Eliab, Abinadab, Shammah, and the rest were rejected. Outwardly, they may have seemed qualified, but God weighed their hearts and found them lacking. Samuel finally asked about the youngest son.

David was a shepherd, which was not a coveted position in Israel. He was also the smallest, perhaps to the point that even his father, Jesse, didn't think his youngest son could be a king. The text implies that David was outwardly unimpressive, even to those who knew him best, yet he was the one God chose!

David would go on to lead an extraordinary life, but we must not miss the truth that every extraordinary event in his life happened through his own ordinariness. David had access to the power of an extraordinary God in part because he did not think he was extraordinary in himself. This is in strong contrast to Saul, who was fully convinced of his own greatness, a folly that led God's Spirit away from him and brought him crashing back down to earth.

What are some snap judgments we tend to make about others based on their appearance or social status?

How does this account warn us against judging others?

Personal Study 2

God's king trusts in the Lord's deliverance.

Read 1 Samuel 17:23-26,34-37.

We pick up the story again in 1 Samuel 17, when Jesse sent David out to visit his brothers on the battlefield. Jesse must not have been impressed with the anointing ceremony because David was still tending sheep while his big brothers were off at war. But as an obedient son, David packed his bags and headed to the front line.

When David arrived, he encountered a jarring situation. The army of Israel was in a stalemate with the army of Philistia. To make matters worse, an enormous Philistine warrior named Goliath would stand before the Israelites and taunt them day after day. When David witnessed this, he asked some nearby Israelite soldiers two questions: First, what was the reward for the man who took down the giant? Second, who did the giant think he was, mouthing off about their God? The second question was the more important of the two because it revealed David's real motivation. He cared about the glory of God.

We see in this story a tragic irony—some of the most discouraging opposition that Christians face comes from the people who *should* be on God's side. Goliath was frightening enough, but there were soldiers doing everything in their power to prevent anyone from stepping out in bold faith. One such soldier was Eliab, David's brother, who scorned him (v. 28). Cowardly people of God are often the biggest obstacle to the mission of God. The real giant in this story was not named Goliath but was the unbelief that dominated the hearts of God's people.

But David was unfazed by the discouragement of people around him. He was the anointed king who trusted in God's power. Besides, he had done his real training in the pasture, and compared to a lion or a bear, Goliath was not terribly impressive.

Maybe there is a reason we are not given a catalog of David's daily events during his time as a shepherd: they would have been the same *every single day*. Walk the sheep from here to there. Lead them to water. Retrieve wandering lamb. Sit. Wait. Repeat. Repeat. Repeat.

But the pasture was also where David honed some of the most vital skills in his life. It was there that he grew in courage, fending off lions and bears from his helpless flock. It was there that he learned humility, cleaning sheep excrement off of his robes and sandals day after day. No wonder Psalm 78:72 says that David "shepherded [the people] with a pure heart and guided them with his skillful hands." An upright heart and a shepherding attitude come from the pasture, not the palace.

This is still what God does with us today. Parents who feel unappreciated—changing diapers for unappreciative infants, for example—experience their own pasture but can do so with joy if they realize that in whatever they do, it is for the Lord (cf. Col. 3:23). Businesspeople often work dead-end jobs, unnoticed even by their own supervisors, but if they work with faithfulness where they are, God often does magnificent things. Students, many of whom are eager to get out into the world and "make a difference," pore over their books, learning material that they may never use, but God is at work in them, forging their character, patience, and integrity. We ought not despise the pasture or resent our suffering—these are God's laboratories for molding our hearts to trust in the Lord's deliverance.

What "pasture" are you in right now or have you experienced in the past?

What does it look like for you to faithfully trust God through that experience?

Personal Study 3

God's king wins an improbable victory for the Lord and His people.

Read 1 Samuel 17:45-51.

The battle scene is gripping. But other than being a fascinating battle story, what exactly is the main lesson to learn in David's triumph over Goliath?

Contemporary audiences love to use this story as an analogy about the underdog: *No matter the odds, you can do it! Just believe in yourself!* Sadly, this misses the point. God does not want us to read this story and come away with a cocky assurance that given the right confidence, we can achieve whatever we set our minds to. Yes, we can glean insight from David's courage and how he overcame insurmountable odds, but that's not the main point of the story. If you are to put yourself in someone's shoes in this story, it should not be David's but those of the people of Israel looking on, hoping David would win the battle. You and I are like the children of Israel, praying for our representative fighter to bring the victory for our side.

The entire scene of David's conflict with Goliath is cast in the light of representative warfare. When David took on Goliath, it was not merely one man against another; this was Israel and Philistia squaring off. What's more, the battle between Israel and Philistia represented the struggle between their gods, as both David and Goliath mentioned in their taunting monologues. Thus, when David won, the rout was on—the Philistines (and their gods) were on the run while Israel (and the one true God) pursued.

David went to the battle line with confidence, not because he found himself particularly worthy but because he saw the battle for what it was—a struggle between the God of Israel and the gods of the world. And when he won, the entire nation of Israel shared in his representative victory, even though they had done nothing to earn it themselves.

We stand in a situation similar to Israel's, in need of a representative to save us from evil. Humanity's greatest and most fundamental problem—the problem behind all of our problems—is our alienation from God due to our sin. And just like Israel, there is nothing any of us can do about that. In fact, there is nothing any of us, of our own accord, even *desire* to do about this.

We are like the hordes of Israelites hiding in our tents, ignoring the threat of Satan, sin, and death. What we need, like Israel, is a representative to take on evil on our behalf. This story prepares the way for God to raise up another King who would accomplish another decisive victory—King Jesus. No one would have expected or picked Him to win the victory, but through His death and resurrection, He is mighty to save, and one day He will come and finally slay the serpent and rescue people from sin and death.

Through this first glimpse into the life of David, we see God's chosen king who honors God and fights for his people. When we step back and look at the big picture of the Bible, we see how God later sent the ultimate King. We would have overlooked Him with our own eyes, but God sent Him for our redemption, the King who achieved a decisive victory for us. This is the King who now sends us out on mission for His kingdom with a message of hope for all who are still trapped in sin and in need of salvation.

Why is it important that David waged his battle against Goliath in the name of the Lord rather than in his own power?

What are some similarities and differences between the story of David and Goliath and the work of Christ?

God Makes a Covenant with David

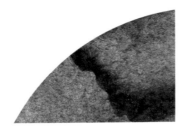

Introducing the Study

David was anointed as the next king of Israel. Though he might not have looked the part, God was grooming His man for this season of ruling, and He demonstrated His commitment to David through David's unlikely victory over Goliath. David was the unexpected warrior and king, and through him we see the shadow of King Jesus, who would eventually win the greatest victory over sin and death.

> What are some unlikely places you have seen God work this past week?

Though he would be the king by which future kings would be measured, David was not the end of the story. Rather, David and the promises God would make to him serve to remind us of the fact that history is moving toward the recognized rule and reign of God's true King–Jesus Christ.

> Why is it important that we not see David as an example of what a king should be but rather see him as a shadow of Jesus to come?

Setting the Context

The mighty Goliath had fallen at the hands of a shepherd boy, and the nation had taken notice. The people rallied to support their new champion in David, and David became a powerful leader in Saul's army. His popularity grew and grew, and all the while, **Saul's resentment of David** grew along with it. On several occasions, Saul tried to kill David, eventually causing David to flee for his life. He only escaped with the aid of Jonathan, Saul's son and David's close friend.

Saul pursued David relentlessly for years. Meanwhile, David gathered around himself a band of outcasts and outlaws as a makeshift army, and they lived life on the run together. During this time, God showed He was with David time and time again, and **David proved his faithfulness** to both God *and* Saul. Though David had the chance to kill Saul and assume the throne on different occasions, he refused to take matters into his own hands and instead was content to see God's plan come to fruition.

> What were some specific occasions this past week when you longed for the full reign of King Jesus to come to fruition?

Eventually, both Saul and his sons were killed in battle. Rather than rejoicing, David mourned and then set about to unify the kingdom that had fractured with the death of Saul. David began his reign as king of Judah when he was thirty years old, and within seven years, he ruled over all of Israel. **"Seeing Jesus in the Kings"** (p. 35) shows how God's work in David's life points forward to His promised King—Jesus.

 What are some of the dangers we might face if we invest our hopes in what an earthly ruler might provide?

✝ CHRIST Connection

God promised David that future kings of Israel would come from his family and that his kingdom would last forever. God kept this promise by sending Jesus as one of David's descendants. All of history is driving toward the day when Jesus, the Son of David, will be recognized by all as the King whose kingdom is everlasting.

Seeing Jesus *in the* Kings

OLD TESTAMENT	NEW TESTAMENT
David Unimpressive Appearance, but God's Chosen King (1 Sam. 16:6-13)	**Jesus** Unimpressive Appearance, but God's Righteous Servant (Isa. 52:13–53:12)
David Defeated Goliath in the Name of the Lord (1 Sam. 17:45)	**Jesus** Saves Us from Sin in the Name of the Lord (Matt. 21:9; Rom. 10:13)
David's Son He Would Build a House for God's Name (2 Sam. 7:13)	**The Son of David** Jesus' Body Is the Sanctuary (John 2:21)
Solomon A Son to God, Disciplined for His Sin (2 Sam. 7:14; 1 Kings 11)	**The Son of God** Jesus Knew No Sin but Died for Ours (1 Pet. 2:21-25)

Continuing the Discussion

▶ Watch this session's video, and then continue the group discussion using the following guide.

In your own words, what is a *covenant*? What made God's covenant with David so special?

Why is it important that we see the fulfillment of God's covenant with David in the rule and reign of Jesus Christ?

As a group, read 2 Samuel 7:8-11a.

Why do you think God reminded David of where he had come from prior to making these promises?

✳ What are some ways God fulfills the promise of rest through Jesus?

In what sense do you long for Jesus to give you rest right now?

David needed to remember that he had not manufactured what was about to happen; rather, it was through God's provision and favor that David would be king. What's more, the rest that would come to God's people would be by His grace alone. Similarly, we can only find true rest when we embrace the work Jesus has done on our behalf and gratefully live inside the grace God gives to us.

As a group, read 2 Samuel 7:11b-17.

Why might it be significant that God said He would build a house for David?

✳ In what specific ways do you see these verses pointing to Jesus?

What does it mean that God is making these promises and not requiring David to make promises in return?

At the beginning of chapter 7, David had been considering building a house for God. But God let David know that He, not David, would build the house. But David's vision was far too small, for God was not going to build a physical structure but an eternal kingdom that would come through one of David's descendants, Jesus the Messiah. This would come to fruition not based on David's strength or faithfulness but by God's grace and His strength to keep His promises.

As a group, read 2 Samuel 7:18-29.

 What characteristics of God did David highlight in this prayer? Why?

How do these verses show us the right way to respond to God's promises to us?

There is no room for pride in the promises of God. What God does, He does out of grace and love, and the proper way to respond is for us to acknowledge His grace and live in a spirit of humility and gratitude for all He has done for us in Christ.

✝ MISSIONAL Application

Record in this space at least one way you will apply the truth of Scripture as a recipient of God's grace and rest through faith in Jesus Christ, God's forever King.

Personal Study 1

God promises to give His people eternal rest.

Read 2 Samuel 7:8-11a.

We catch up with David in 2 Samuel 7, where he was living large as the established king of Israel. From his palatial balcony, David looked down and saw the travel-worn tabernacle that served as God's house. So David made a commitment to build God a beautiful new house. In response to David's seemingly generous act, God flipped David's script.

Before God issued one of the most notable promises in the Old Testament to David, He referred back to recent history to remind David how he got where he was. God, not David, was the provider. Look at the reminders He gave David:

• "I took you from the pasture."

• "I have been with you."

• "I have destroyed all your enemies before you."

God reminded David that every step of the way—from the pasture to the palace—Hewas orchestrating David's steps. In keeping with a common pattern in Scripture, God reminded David of His faithfulness before He made His promise.

When we read this passage, we ought to ask ourselves: *Are we not just as quick as David to consider ourselves independent and self-sufficient? Have we forgotten how God has brought us to the place we are now?* In times of plenty, we are less likely to throw ourselves on the mercy of God than when times are difficult.

Grace—it seems so simple. It's a gift, costly for the giver but free for the recipient. Yet this is where so many people stumble. We're hard-wired to ask: "How much is *enough*? How often do I need to come to church? How much money do I have to give?" These questions will *never* get you to the gospel. The gospel begins with God's extravagant gift. Jesus' blood—and Jesus' blood alone—is *enough* for your weary, guilty soul.

Christianity is not about you living a good life and then giving your record to God; it is about Jesus living the perfect life and then giving His record to you as a gift. He lived the life we were supposed to live and died the death we should have died. His life is ours, but only if we receive it. The story of God flipping the script and making a promise to King David sets the stage for that glorious gospel.

With David's perspective corrected, God began giving promises to David. The first three conclude with God declaring that peace will come to Israel. Israel had been in wars and battles for many years, so this was welcome news. And if we are honest, we all admit we want a place to rest—a place of security, no longer worrying if something bad or tragic is just around the corner.

For the Christian, our rest is found in Jesus Christ. In John 15:9, Jesus commanded us to make our home in Him. His name and His presence are the "rest" we've been looking for. He who keeps His word is sure to make good on the promise to grant rest to His followers (Matt. 11:28). When we make our home in Him, He will display His glory through us to the world.

How does the gospel of Jesus Christ grant rest to those who believe it?

How does our inability to rest in Christ hinder our witness?

Personal Study 2

God promises to establish an eternal kingdom.

Read 2 Samuel 7:11b-16.

God lifted David's eyes to see something amazing. David had been thinking of building God a house. But what God offered to do instead would never have entered David's mind as something to ask for.

David's desire to build God a house might seem odd to contemporary readers, but it was a common practice in the ancient world. King Tut, for instance, built a temple for the Egyptian god Amon-Ra. In exchange, Amon-Ra allegedly proclaimed that King Tut would rule a kingdom that spanned the globe and lasted for millions of years. (He fell just a few thousand miles and a few million years short.)

But note the order: (1) a king builds a temple for a god; (2) the temple makes the god famous; (3) the god thanks the king by blessing his kingdom. That's the order of every religion in the world: work hard for me and I'll work hard for you. But God rejected that idea and reversed it. Essentially, God said to David: "My power establishes you, and you will always be My debtor. Your life will be lived in grateful response to Me." The house that God would build would not bear the inscription "Built by David for God" but "Built by God for David."

This promise for God to build David an eternal house is a promise that ultimately refers to the Messiah who would come and reign forever. But one detail immediately strikes a lot of readers as odd: "When he does wrong..." If we're talking about Jesus here (which we are), then what is this about iniquity? Jesus never sinned!

It is helpful to remember that most biblical prophecies have a dual meaning. There is an *immediate* meaning, and then there is an *ultimate* one. From the perspective of the prophets, of course, it was often difficult to untie the two, but they remain distinct. Think of it like the experience of seeing a mountain range in the distance. When you first spot it, you might see two distinct peaks seemingly right next to each other. It's only as you get closer that you see these peaks are miles apart.

The first fulfillment of this prophecy was David's biological son Solomon. Solomon's name literally means "rest," so in many ways he would exemplify this promise. His reign would extend *rest* throughout Israel, and it would be on his watch that Israel constructed the temple (the subject of a later session). Still, Solomon would do some patently foolish things. Even so, God would keep His promise and would not strip the kingdom from him completely.

Yet this prophecy points *through* Solomon to another king—Jesus. He was the descendant of David whose kingdom would last; His temple was His own body and, by extension, the church. Unlike Solomon, Jesus would not need to be disciplined with the stripes of men. Instead, He would be bruised for *our* iniquity, and by His stripes, we would be healed (Isa. 53:5). The *real* Son of David would build the *real* temple of God and establish God's *real* presence with His people forever. And He would not just be David's son. He would be God's own Son, building the house of salvation for God's people on earth *all by Himself.*

Wrap your head around that—God would build His own house, and He would *become* the house He promised to build. *In Jesus, God would be the fulfillment to His own promise.*

Why do you think it is important that God promised to reign through a human being?

In what ways does the church fulfill the role of being God's temple?

Personal Study 3

We respond to God's promise with gratitude and humility.

Read 2 Samuel 7:18-29.

This messianic promise was astounding—so astounding, in fact, that we may be tempted to miss David's response. But here we see the story come full circle. David began this discussion wanting to *go* and *build* for God, but he ended it by sitting, wondering, knowing, pondering, adoring, and then exalting the King who deserves all glory.

This is the key to salvation. Asking "How much is *enough* for God?" is the wrong starting point. Instead, salvation starts with knowing what God has already done, which leaves us sitting in stunned awe in the presence of God. Yes, trusting Christ will lead you to *do* things for God. But everything you do is only ever a grateful *response* to what He's already done for you.

We often think that the world is supposed to look at Christians and say, "What impressive works they've done! They must really love God." But as God shows us here, our witness to the world should leave them saying, "Wow, what great things *God* has done *for them!*"

We Christians are not primarily role models. We are trophies, works of art that demonstrate God's saving power. No one admires a trophy for having done something great; they recognize that the trophy represents *someone* having done something great. Our lives are supposed to burn brightly with evidence of God's miraculous greatness. And ironically, the more we steep ourselves in the finished work of Christ, the more we will find His Spirit rising up within us. The fire to *do* in the Christian life comes only from being soaked in the fuel of what He has *done*.

This story is all about God's house, God's kingdom, God's unfolding drama. But the wonder of it all is that we are invited to share in that story. God calls us first to behold Him in wonder, but He also commissions us to go and tell.

What God told David is just as true for us. Our kingdoms will fail. Our businesses will fail. Our loftiest ambitions will fail. Even our families will not last forever. Jesus is the only thing that will last forever. And the greatest privilege of our lives is asking God to show us where we can join Jesus. He doesn't need us, but He will use us for eternal value. He can make our minuscule lives into something beautiful, precious, and everlasting. For far too many of us, our lives are just so small. We think of God as a personal assistant, someone to get us out of a jam. What He desires for us is so much bigger, so much richer, so much more profound than any of us realize.

But that greatness begins in humility. It is one of the great paradoxes of the Christian faith: If you desire greatness for yourself, God will oppose you, but if you desire God to be great, your life will have eternal value and miraculous power. Don't waste your life building houses for yourself, or even building houses for God. Rest in His all-sufficient work, and answer Him when He calls.

In what ways do ingratitude and pride hinder us in our mission?

Why are gratitude and humility necessary qualities for us as we share the gospel?

David Sins and Is Restored

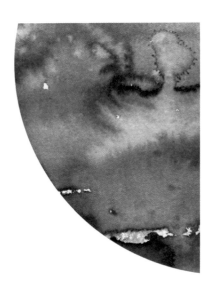
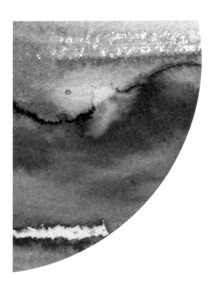

Introducing the Study

David became the greatest king of Israel. He ruled God's people with integrity as a shepherd would look after his flock, and during his reign Israel enjoyed prosperity and favor. David lived in light of God's kindness to him and his people, bolstered by God's promise to establish an everlasting kingdom through him that would ultimately be fulfilled by Jesus.

 In what ways does Jesus bring prosperity and security that no earthly king ever could?

Yes, David was a great king. And yet, like any other human being, David fell short of God's standard. No matter how high we might rise in human terms, not one of us is ever beyond sin. In fact, the question is not whether we will sin but rather how we will respond in light of the gospel when we do.

What are some reasons we might consider ourselves beyond the reach of temptation and sin?

Setting the Context

After establishing his reign in Israel, **David enjoyed a period of great success.** Nation after nation fell before David and the Israelite army, and God was with them in whatever they did. With each victory, the borders of Israel became more and more secure. Meanwhile, David both privately and publicly acknowledged that the battle belonged to the Lord.

It was also during this time that **David honored a promise** he had made to his friend Jonathan many years before. In a powerful display of mercy and grace, David sought out Jonathan's heir, Mephibosheth, and showed kindness to him, giving him a seat at the king's table for the sake of Jonathan. This was unusual, gracious, and kind because it was customary for a king to eliminate any potential threats to his throne as he reigned.

 What are some ways our priorities ought to be distinct from the world's because we live under the reign of Jesus?

Perhaps because of his military victories, however, David grew lax in his spiritual commitment. **"David's Enemies"** (p. 47) highlights some of the ways David had seen God's blessing and protection. But in spite of God's anointing and provision, David succumbed to a most insidious enemy—himself—showing us that no one is beyond the reach of temptation and sin; even the mighty are not immune from falling.

What are some of the dangers in considering ourselves beyond temptation and sin?

✝ CHRIST Connection

Even David, the greatest of Israel's kings and the man after God's own heart, was a sinner who needed to repent and be redeemed. In the story of David, we recognize that we all need forgiveness through the sacrifice of the perfect King, who would take upon Himself the punishment our sins deserve.

David's *Enemies*

Enemy's THREAT	David's ACTION	God's PROVISION
Goliath, a Giant Defied the armies of the living God (1 Sam. 17:8-10,26)	Defeated Goliath with a sling and a stone; with no sword of his own, he struck him down and killed him (1 Sam. 17:48-51)	The Lord handed Goliath over to David (1 Sam. 17:45-47)
King Saul Tried to kill David with his spear and his army (1 Sam. 18–26)	Fled from Saul and twice restrained himself from killing Saul, the Lord's anointed (1 Sam. 24; 26)	The Lord delivered David from the hand of Saul (2 Sam. 12:7)
The Philistines Searched for King David to kill him (2 Sam. 5:17-18)	Went to war with the Philistines and defeated them (2 Sam. 5:20-25)	The Lord handed the Philistines over to David (2 Sam. 5:19,24)
David, Himself Sinned against the Lord by committing adultery and murder (2 Sam. 11)	When confronted by the prophet Nathan, he confessed his sin and repented (2 Sam. 12:1-13)	The Lord took away his sin; he would not die, though his son would, and rebellion would come from his own family (2 Sam. 12:10-14)

Continuing the Discussion

Watch this session's video, and then continue the group discussion using the following guide.

What are some things we can learn about temptation based on the story of David and Bathsheba?

How do you see the progression of sin in this story? How have you seen that play out around you?

As a group, read 2 Samuel 11:1-5.

How did this sin begin? Why is that important to recognize?

How should we as Christians work to protect ourselves from compromising situations like this?

Why do you think one sin tends to lead to more sin?

At the start of the spring, David sent Joab and his troops to fight the Ammonites while he remained behind in Jerusalem. As a result, David found himself idle, and in his idleness, he was enticed by what he saw. At any point, David could have chosen to turn away from sin, and yet, he continued to take steps forward in his sinful progression.

As a group, read 2 Samuel 11:6-17.

How are Uriah and David presented as opposites in these verses?

Who was affected by David's sin, both directly and indirectly? What can you say about the effect of sin based on this?

How does the gospel help us to acknowledge our sin and repent of it?

When David's sin seemed to trap him, instead of repenting and acknowledging it, he tried to cover it up. David, like Adam and Eve before him, hid from what he had done, and the consequences were severe. Because we believe the gospel, we are free to take a different road. When we sin, we can acknowledge our sin and turn back to God, knowing He accepts us in Christ, instead of continuing in a downward spiral.

As a group, read Psalm 51:4-10.

 How is David's attitude toward his sin in this psalm different than in the narrative account?

In what ways does this psalm give us a blueprint for how to respond to our own sin?

Written after the death of his child, David acknowledged his sin before God. He did not offer explanation or self-justification, just the simple confession of what he had done. He also praised God knowing that when we sin, God's grace abounds.

✛ MISSIONAL Application

Record in this space at least one way you will apply the truth of Scripture as a repentant and forgiven sinner through faith in Jesus Christ.

Personal Study 1

The king commits sin.

Read 2 Samuel 11:1-5.

Sin doesn't exist in a vacuum. A number of factors can contribute to producing temptation in our minds and hearts and lead us further into sin. As we examine David's sin, we can gain insight into how we give in to our own sinful desires.

The first thing we should note about King David's path toward sin is that this temptation came after he had received the blessing of God. At this point in the biblical narrative, the kingdom of Israel is firmly established. David is at the height of his popularity. In the preceding chapters, David emerged as the victor of many battles. We tend to think that adversity is what precedes sinful behavior, as if sin becomes merely an escape from reality. But blessing can be just as dangerous.

The danger in times of blessing is that we forget just how dependent we are on God. When life overflows with goodness, it is easy to assume we have caused it. So God gets pushed to the periphery. This is why the author of Proverbs 30 prayed to God, "Give me neither poverty nor wealth," but rather: "Feed me with the food I need. Otherwise, I might have too much and deny you, saying, 'Who is the LORD?'" (vv. 8-9). The more self-sufficient we feel, the closer we are to disaster. As the apostle Paul said, "Whoever thinks he stands must be careful not to fall" (1 Cor. 10:12).

A second critical element of David's temptation is that he was disengaged from his work. The king had just sent Joab and the whole army out to battle, but David stayed back. David the warrior had become David the vacationer, and his lack of engagement made him susceptible to cheap thrills.

One way to successfully resist the enticements of this world isn't by force of will. It's to be busy with a higher purpose. For many people, their lives are so empty, so pointless, so devoid of something more, that the excitement of sexual sin promises a fulfillment they desperately crave. It's not always that sin is incredibly alluring; it's often that we're so unbelievably bored. We simply weren't designed to live our lives on the sidelines. Only a vision of what God has done for you in the gospel will keep you from giving your soul away to idols.

The third element of this temptation is that David was in the place where he could be tempted. It is far easier to avoid temptation than it is to resist sin. Let's be clear: resisting sin is important, immensely so. We must cultivate a habit of coming face to face with temptation and still resisting sin. But the world throws enough temptation our way; do we really need to seek out more of it?

David's dark road continued. His descent into sin wasn't immediate, and even here, we see how he was given a chance to escape. "Isn't this Eliam's daughter?" someone told him. "Isn't that Uriah's wife?" Why these details? This is the author pointing out to us—even if David didn't quite catch it—that Bathsheba was someone's wife, someone's daughter. The anonymous person who answered David was trying to say, ever so subtly, "David, I know what you're thinking. And someone is going to get hurt."

Sin hurts people. It affects someone's mother, someone's daughter, someone's son—even if that someone is just you. God's rules, we have to remember, are never arbitrary. They are given to us for His glory and our good, to show us the most life-giving way of interacting with others. God doesn't want to keep us from sinning because He's out to ruin our fun. He wants to keep us from sinning because He knows how deeply it will wound us and others. Sin disintegrates. Sin wounds. Every time. Without fail.

What are the blessings God has provided you that are most likely to make you forget your dependence on Him, if you let them?

What are the most vulnerable times and places where you are most likely to face temptation?

Personal Study 2

The king compounds sin.

Read 2 Samuel 11:6-17.

As the story unfolds, we see David at his most ingenious—and at his most devious—as he schemed and hatched plans to hide his sin.

Plan A was an obvious one, but a difficult one to accomplish: David attempted to trick Uriah into thinking the baby was his.

At any other time of year, this might not have seemed too difficult. But Uriah, you'll recall, was miles away fighting David's battles. So David needed to "create a moment." He invited Uriah home from battle, asked for a briefing on the war, and then sent him home. David thought he had it covered.

But he was wrong. Uriah was a noble man, and he was thinking of all his comrades sleeping in the field. They didn't have the pleasure of sleeping in their own bed and being with their wives. So Uriah camped out with the palace guards for a night. Imagine how convicting that was for David.

David, however, wasn't a quitter. He plotted Plan B, which was an upgrade on Plan A. It now included getting Uriah drunk, thereby lowering his inhibitions. Uriah, despite his nobility, walked right into David's plot. But still, he would not go home, choosing instead to sleep again among David's servants. Strike two for David.

So David started Plan C. He wrote a note to Joab that told him to put Uriah in the front of the battle and to abandon him. It was a death sentence for Uriah, *and Uriah himself carried the letter to Joab*. In the end, David's plan succeeded. Uriah died in battle, David was free to openly marry Bathsheba, and it looked like David was going to get away with his sin.

But then comes the chilling end to the chapter: "The LORD considered what David had done to be evil" (2 Sam. 11:27). No one else may have seen what truly happened. David may have convinced himself that it was all behind him. But God's eyes were watching. They always are.

This is the insidious nature of sin—it begets more and more. What starts with a glance turns into a thought which turns into an action which turns into a lie to cover it all up, and so the progression continues. In the New Testament, James warned believers about this slow but steady downward spiral: "But each person is tempted when he is drawn away and enticed by his own evil desire. Then after desire has conceived, it gives birth to sin, and when sin is fully grown, it gives birth to death" (Jas. 1:14-15).

David's life from this point forward began to unravel. Sin can always be forgiven. As we will see in a moment, David came to God and received healing for what he had done. But we can't always undo the damage caused by our sin. Sin is a plague—by its very nature, it destroys. The whispers of sin that promise joy are lies, and the end of that road is disaster.

When have you tried to cover up sin? What happened?

What are some consequences you have experienced because of your sin?

What are some consequences others have experienced because of your sin?

Personal Study 3

The king confesses sin.

Read Psalm 51:4-10.

Few of us have sinned as egregiously as David did—in adultery and murder—but we all sin. And every one of us is capable of David's heinous crimes. But no matter the sin, there is only one true remedy for it, and that is to repent. The question is not "Do you sin?" The question is "What do you do *after* you sin?"

In God's kindness, He chose to expose what David had covered up. God sent the prophet Nathan to remind David that although he thought he had gotten away with everything, God wouldn't let it end there. And in a moment of profound humility, David finally came clean. The result was one of the most beautiful and exemplary songs in Scripture—Psalm 51. In this psalm, David shows us the keys to gospel-centered repentance and confession.

David began precisely where he should, by centering on God's grace. So must we, for our sole hope in repentance is the mercy of God. Nothing in this prayer suggests that David came to God looking to make a deal. He was not bargaining with God, trying to commute his sentence. He was not trying to explain away his sin. He was not even promising to do better in the future. No, David appealed to God on the only ground that won't crumble, the ground of God's grace.

Second, gospel-centered repentance owns the truth that the sin we commit is deeply inherent to who we are. When we're caught in our sin, our natural inclination is to explain it away: "I'm not really as bad as all that," we want to say. "It was just a moment of weakness." But David went the complete opposite direction. He owned not only his specific act of sin but his inherent sinfulness.

Finally, this prayer shows us repentance is first directed toward God because our sin is first against God. But here's where we might be confused. "Against you—you alone—I have sinned," David said. Really? Against God *alone*? What about Bathsheba? Or Uriah? On the face of it, this doesn't make sense, but it's actually the heart of David's entire prayer.

David realized that his sin began as a sin against God. What was it about Bathsheba that David wanted? Was it the feeling of power? Her beauty? A moment of physical pleasure? Ultimately, David wasn't swept away because he wanted something specific. David was seduced by Bathsheba's beauty because he was no longer captivated by God's.

All of our sin starts as a dissolution in our relationship with God. We grow dissatisfied with what God has given us, as we doubt His goodness toward us. So we start to feel God's boundaries as restrictive, not life-giving. That means the way to deal with sin in our lives isn't merely to suppress the sin; it's to increase our delight in God so that we love Him more than we love the sin. The only way to overcome sinful urges is not by learning to love them less but by learning to love God more.

Many of us don't realize how large and majestic is our God. But think, the bloody cross was the price for our sin. Jesus didn't have to die because of what we did to each other but because of what we did to God. Sin should thus upset us not just because of its consequences but because it stands against our holy God; otherwise, our repentance will only be a smokescreen.

What are some ways we "water down" repentance by bargaining with God or by explaining away our mistakes?

How does true repentance differ from being sorry we were caught or from experiencing sin's consequences?

What happens when we minimize the severity of our rebellion against God?

God Gives Solomon Wisdom

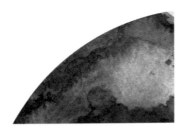
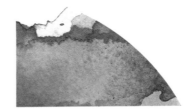

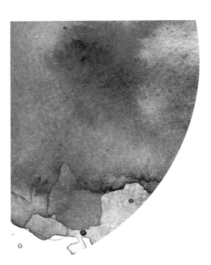

Introducing the Study

Despite being chosen by God and enjoying tremendous victory as a king, David shows us the danger of lurking sin and how we are all prone to its power in our lives. But at the same time, David also provides a model for repentance. David's fall was great, but when he was confronted, he humbled himself before God, reminding us that we can have confidence that we will be forgiven because of the great grace of our God.

 What are some of the marks of true repentance?

Despite his greatness, David was still an earthly king, as was his son Solomon, the heir to the throne. Though both enjoyed great prosperity and favor during their reigns, both were still ultimately dependent on God for everything they needed—including forgiveness of their sin. Even Solomon, who reigned with great wisdom and insight, only did so because God granted it to him. Once again, we are reminded of our need for a greater king, a perfect king—King Jesus, who never fails His Father or His people.

> What are some ways we might guard our hearts from drifting toward independence from God?

Setting the Context

David was a great king. And yet, the latter years of his life read more like a tragedy. Despite all his military and political struggles, the greatest turmoil for David would come through his own family. First, **the child David and Bathsheba conceived died** while still an infant as a consequence of his sin.

Next, among David's children from other wives, **Amnon** was infatuated with his half-sister Tamar, and his desire drove him to rape her. When Absalom, Tamar's brother, learned what happened, he was enraged and eventually killed Amnon. After murdering his brother, he fled the country.

David mourned his son, but after some time, he allowed **Absalom** to come home, only to have Absalom mount a revolt against him to seize the throne. Though the rebellion was eventually quashed, David bore witness to the death of yet another one of his sons.

> How do we see the effects of David's sin in the actions of his children?

After reigning for forty years, near the end of his days, David named Solomon, a second son born to him and Bathsheba, as his successor. **"Solomon's Wisdom"** (p. 59) highlights how this son, at least for a time, demonstrated extraordinary wisdom. He asked for wisdom from God because he recognized his need to depend upon the Lord in order to lead his people well.

 Why do you think it's so easy for us to forget that we need to depend upon God?

✝ CHRIST Connection

Solomon reigned with great wisdom and insight, yet he was still an imperfect king who needed God's forgiveness. Solomon foreshadows the coming of a greater king—Jesus, in whom is hidden "all the treasures of wisdom and knowledge" (Col. 2:3).

Solomon's *Wisdom*

Wisdom Literature	Style	Purpose	Points to Jesus
Proverbs	A few extended wisdom poems, but largely consists of unrelated proverbs strung together—proverbs are general rules, not absolute promises	Gives positive and negative principles for successful living in the world God has created, chiefly the need to "fear the Lord" (Prov. 1:7)	All the treasures of wisdom and knowledge are found in Jesus Christ, who created all things and holds all things together (Col. 1:15-17; 2:3)
Ecclesiastes	A mixture of poetry and prose; overtly pessimistic about life "under the sun," or apart from God	Explains that the meaning of life is to fear God and keep His commandments (Eccl. 12:13)	To fear God is to know Him and the One He has sent—Jesus (John 17:3); we are to obey Him and teach others to do the same (Matt. 28:18-20)
Song of Solomon, or Song of Songs	A song composed entirely of Hebrew poetry, featuring a bride, a groom, and a chorus of "friends"	Explains that a husband and a wife should enjoy the sexual dimension of their relationship	This ideal romance, as with every marriage, is a picture of the greater relationship between Christ and His bride, the church (Eph. 5:22-33)

Continuing the Discussion

 Watch this session's video, and then continue the group discussion using the following guide.

How would you define *wisdom*?

What are some differences between the wisdom that comes from God and the wisdom of the world?

As a group, read 1 Kings 3:5-9.

Based on this passage, what are some of the things Solomon believed to be true about God and about himself?

Why is God the only true source of wisdom?

What are some areas of your life right now in which you desperately need the wisdom of the Lord?

One of Solomon's great characteristics displayed here at the beginning of his reign was a knowledge of what he lacked. Solomon recognized the task before him, and he knew that only through God's help would he be able to rule with wisdom. We too have been given tasks by God, though perhaps not ruling a kingdom. We also need wisdom to parent, to work, and to make daily decisions that display the gospel in our culture.

As a group, read 1 Kings 3:10-15.

Why do you think this request pleased the Lord?

Why is wisdom such a necessary quality for anyone in authority?

What does God's response teach you about what He values in His people?

Rather than asking for something that would selfishly fulfill a temporal desire, Solomon humbly asked to be equipped for what God had tasked him to do. This is the kind of attitude God honors—faithful dependence on God by one who wants to walk in His will, while acknowledging the inability to do so apart from God's help.

As a group, read 1 Kings 3:16-28.

What led to this ruling by Solomon?

Why is this a good example of wisdom being exercised?

✱ Why is it important, as we see in verse 28, that wisdom leads to justice?

Wisdom is about real life. We exercise wisdom when we are confronted with real life circumstances in which we must make a choice. God doesn't intend for us to be paralyzed by indecision but rather that we make daily choices from His wisdom that He has given us. In so doing, we seek justice for all people in our spheres of influence.

✝ MISSIONAL Application

Record in this space at least one way you will apply the truth of Scripture as a recipient of the wisdom of God in Jesus Christ.

Personal Study 1

The king requests wisdom.

Read 1 Kings 3:5-9.

God appeared to Solomon in a vision and said: "Ask. What should I give you?" (v. 5).
Most of us would love for God to ask us this question. Our minds would immediately
consider all the possibilities; all of what we have ever wanted would be ready to fall
from our lips. Solomon could have asked for all sorts of things as well, but he chose
to request wisdom.

Notice first how Solomon saw himself as he prayed. He began by confessing that he
was "just a youth with no experience in leadership" (v. 7). He admitted that he had
no business being the king of such a great people. In addition, he recognized that he
was there only by divine appointment: "You have now made your servant king in my
father David's place" (v. 7). God placed him there. It was an act of God's grace.

Seeing himself and his weaknesses, Solomon felt compelled to ask for the one thing
he knew he could not live without—God's wisdom. Solomon was living out what he
would write some years later: "Trust in the LORD with all your heart, and do not rely
on your own understanding; in all your ways know him, and he will make your paths
straight. Don't be wise in your own eyes; fear the LORD and turn away from evil"
(Prov. 3:5-7).

Seeing ourselves as we truly are should drive us to beg God for His wisdom as
well. Recognizing God's grace in our lives and admitting that the task before us
is impossible in our own strength humbles us and causes us to reach out for divine
wisdom. When we think too highly of ourselves, we are in danger of walking in
our own wisdom and strength, which will lead to failure (see John 15:5-6).

So Solomon asked for God's wisdom so he could lead God's people well. He would be
the direct recipient of this gift from God, but his intention was to use this wisdom to
lead the people of Israel with justice and equity. His motivation for wanting wisdom
was others-centered, not self-centered. That's one reason why his prayer pleased
the Lord.

Similar to Solomon, God gives us wisdom so we can relate rightly to those around us. We need wisdom to be godly friends, neighbors, husbands, wives, parents, bosses, employees, and citizens.

James, the half-brother of Jesus, once offered a stark warning about asking for things only for ourselves when he wrote: "You desire and do not have. You murder and covet and cannot obtain. You fight and wage war. You do not have because you do not ask. You ask and don't receive because you ask with wrong motives, so that you may spend it on your pleasures" (Jas. 4:2-3). Often we want God to give us things because of what it does for us. Our comfort and our pleasure are at the center of our minds. But Solomon made a request because he had a godly desire to bless and lead others. And that should be the beat of our heart as well.

In what areas of your life are you prone to feel self-sufficient?

In what areas would you most likely lean on your own understanding and not ask for God's wisdom?

In what relationships in your life do you most need God's wisdom right now? Why?

Personal Study 2

The king receives wisdom.

Read 1 Kings 3:10-15.

Solomon's request pleased the Lord. Why? Because in his request, Solomon acknowledged that God's ways are right, and by requesting wisdom, Solomon was implicitly expressing His desire to walk in the ways of God and lead others to do the same.

How can we know that our requests will please the Lord like this? We measure them by what we know to be God's will. We know that God wants us to walk in purity, love our enemies, and give generously. But we also know that in and of ourselves, we lack the internal resources to do any of these things. When we ask for these things, which we know are God's will, we will find God ready to provide.

Requesting God's wisdom should be a regular part of our prayers as we encounter various situations that reveal our need for it. And as we pray, we can be confident that God wants to grant our request for wisdom just as He did with Solomon. While we may not compose three thousand proverbs, we can trust God for wisdom as we talk to our neighbor about the gospel. We can wisely respond to our spouse who may be walking through a difficult season. We can navigate the rocky terrain of life as we receive the wisdom God provides.

This is why Solomon wrote so elegantly about pursuing wisdom: "Happy is a man who finds wisdom and who acquires understanding, for she is more profitable than silver, and her revenue is better than gold. She is more precious than jewels; nothing you desire can equal her. Long life is in her right hand; in her left, riches and honor. Her ways are pleasant, and all her paths, peaceful. She is a tree of life to those who embrace her, and those who hold on to her are happy" (Prov. 3:13-18).

How true this is! We need wisdom more than we might realize. Too often we think that money, power, and approval are what we need most. But Solomon's life is evidence that when all is said and done, it is wisdom from God that aids us best in our time of need. We must fight to believe this.

One area we especially need wisdom in is the area of mission. God gives us wisdom so we can better announce the gospel to the world. In other words, *wisdom is for mission!*

If we are going to be salt and light in the world, we need wisdom. We need it to relate rightly to the non-Christians around us. We need it to show how money, power, and pleasure are not what matter most in this life. We need it as we interact with those who are skeptical or even hostile to Christianity. This is why Paul said, "Act wisely toward outsiders, making the most of the time" (Col. 4:5). It was because of Solomon's wisdom, granted by God, that people came from everywhere to hear from him (see 1 Kings 4:34).

Wisdom makes us appealing and attractive to those around us. The world needs to see God-given wisdom. They need to see Christians walking wisely when it comes to money, parenting, and suffering. They need to see that the gospel has fully equipped us and empowered us to live righteous and upright lives in this world (Titus 2:11-13).

Think of your neighborhood. You are likely surrounded by people who do not know the Lord—and seem to have no desire to do so. You need wisdom to know how to talk with these men, women, and children and to live winsomely around them. They need to see wisdom on display in your life as you interact with your family and as you talk about the world. We need wisdom in order to serve, bless, and love those around us.

What are some ways you can celebrate God's wisdom in your life?

How would you explain to someone that wisdom is more valuable than wealth, power, or approval?

Personal Study 3

The king exercises wisdom.

Read 1 Kings 3:16-28.

After Solomon's prayer for wisdom, he was confronted with a situation that tested the depth of understanding God had given him. Two prostitutes approached the king to resolve a dispute. They both claimed that a baby belonged to them, and they had come to the king for a ruling.

This story shows that God truly answered the prayer of Solomon. The people of Israel saw their king reigning in wisdom and discernment in a way that could only be attributed to God. Here we have proof that God fulfilled His promise to Solomon, a reminder of God's faithfulness. This is the kind of God we serve, One who does what He says He will do.

This story shows us that we should not only ask for God's wisdom—we should expect it! James reminded us of this when he wrote: "Now if any of you lacks wisdom, he should ask God—who gives to all generously and ungrudgingly—and it will be given to him. But let him ask in faith without doubting. For the doubter is like the surging sea, driven and tossed by the wind" (Jas. 1:5-6). That is God's wisdom at work. He gives it generously as we pursue Him by faith.

Parents understand the importance of asking for something. How tragic would it be if our children needed our help but failed to ask us for fear we would not grant it! Our God is a prayer-answering God. He responds to our cries for wisdom because it is something He loves to grant.

Jesus said: "Who among you, if his son asks him for bread, will give him a stone? Or if he asks for a fish, will give him a snake? If you then, who are evil, know how to give good gifts to your children, how much more will your Father in heaven give good things to those who ask him" (Matt. 7:9-11). Our God delights to see His people walk in wisdom for His glory and our good, which is why He is so eager to grant it when we ask Him for it.

It is highly unlikely we will be confronted with the same situation as Solomon, but we know we will face problems that lack a clear solution. For instance, a business deal comes your way that could change your life dramatically, yet it requires moving your family across the country. What do you do? Or one day your child asks you why his classmate has two mothers. What do you say? How do you respond?

There are countless situations in which we need wisdom. Thankfully, our God is the all-wise God. He alone has all wisdom and understanding. Let us go to Him and expect that He will respond to us.

When have you sensed the Lord granting you wisdom as you gave advice to someone or as you made a decision?

What are some specific arenas in life in which you should be regularly asking for God's wisdom?

The Temple Is Built

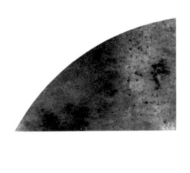
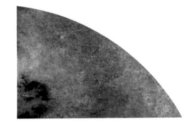
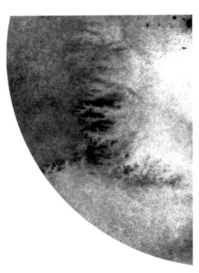
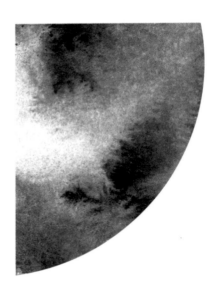

Introducing the Study

After God granted his request, Solomon's wisdom became known far and wide. He was renowned for his ability to judge and rule his people. God was generous with his wisdom toward Solomon, and as God's children, we are promised that He will be similarly generous with us when we humbly ask for wisdom.

> **What are some practices you can incorporate into your life that will help you live with wisdom?**

One of the lasting contributions Solomon would make to God's people and the story of redemption would be the construction of God's temple. Solomon was careful to obey the instructions for building the temple in a way that magnified the greatness of God. And yet, this physical structure was only a shadow of God's true dwelling place that was to come—Jesus Christ.

 How do you think the temple points us to Jesus?

Setting the Context

Solomon's fame soon spread throughout the earth. He was regarded as the wisest man in the world, and emissaries from all over came to Israel to seek his counsel. Solomon's kingdom grew with his prestige, and as God had promised, Solomon grew in wealth and power. His kingdom was one of excess and prosperity, and that prosperity extended to everyone in the kingdom. What's more, Solomon was a prolific student and writer. He studied zoology, biology, and botany as well as recording thousands of proverbs and songs.

> Why does God's wisdom have an impact on fields of study beyond just theology and ethics?

Solomon had in mind one particular task with which to utilize his wisdom. Years earlier, Solomon's father, David, had endeavored to build a house for God—**a temple as a tribute to God's great name and renown**. But God told David that this task was not meant for him; instead, his son Solomon would be the one to build the temple. Solomon found himself in a position with near unlimited resources at his disposal, and so it came time for him to fulfill what God had told David his son would do. The king set about building the temple of God. **"The Temple"** (p. 71) explains how this structure served God's will for His glory and His mission.

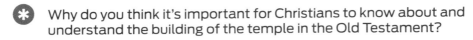 Why do you think it's important for Christians to know about and understand the building of the temple in the Old Testament?

CHRIST Connection

The temple was to be a place where the name of God would be upheld and the presence of God would be experienced so that the nations would know the Lord is God. Jesus spoke of Himself as God's Temple, and in His life, death, and resurrection, He upheld God's name, embodied God's presence, and extended God's mission.

The **Temple**

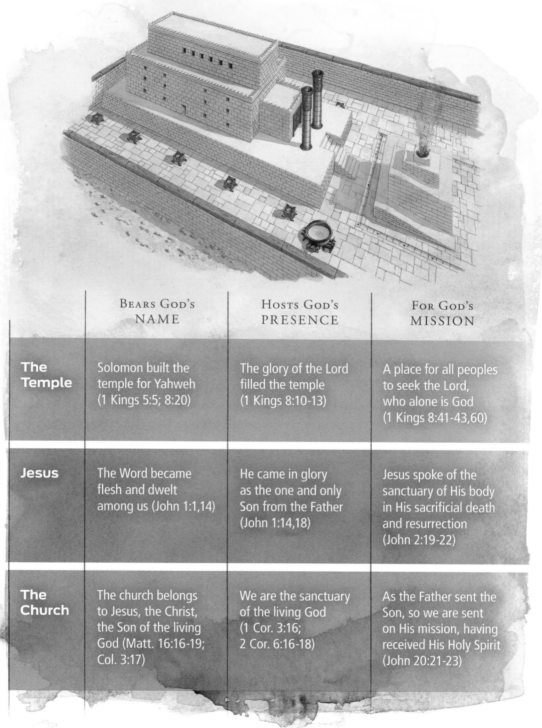

	BEARS GOD'S NAME	HOSTS GOD'S PRESENCE	FOR GOD'S MISSION
The Temple	Solomon built the temple for Yahweh (1 Kings 5:5; 8:20)	The glory of the Lord filled the temple (1 Kings 8:10-13)	A place for all peoples to seek the Lord, who alone is God (1 Kings 8:41-43,60)
Jesus	The Word became flesh and dwelt among us (John 1:1,14)	He came in glory as the one and only Son from the Father (John 1:14,18)	Jesus spoke of the sanctuary of His body in His sacrificial death and resurrection (John 2:19-22)
The Church	The church belongs to Jesus, the Christ, the Son of the living God (Matt. 16:16-19; Col. 3:17)	We are the sanctuary of the living God (1 Cor. 3:16; 2 Cor. 6:16-18)	As the Father sent the Son, so we are sent on His mission, having received His Holy Spirit (John 20:21-23)

Continuing the Discussion

▶ Watch this session's video, and then continue the group discussion using the following guide.

What are some ways the temple communicated the holiness of God?

How should our knowledge of Christ change the way we think about the temple?

As a group, read 1 Kings 5:1-5.

Why, according to these verses, was Solomon going to build the temple?

✳ How would the building of the temple magnify the name of God?

Solomon knew that his father, David, was unable to build the temple because of the warfare that surrounded his life. Instead, because Solomon's reign was marked by peace and prosperity, he would engage in this work. The temple was meant to be a structure that paid honor to God. It was intended to be a place where people from all over the world would come to meet with and worship the one true God.

As a group, read 1 Kings 8:10-14.

What does this description of the temple dedication remind you of from earlier in the Old Testament?

What attributes of God do you see magnified in this description?

✳ What are some proper ways to respond to the glory of the Lord?

It would be a mistake to think that the temple could fully house the presence of God. After all, the universe itself cannot contain all of God's glory because He is infinite and omnipresent; how could He possibly live in the temple that was so small by comparison? The temple was only a shadow of what was to come. God was not going to dwell ultimately within a temple built by the hands of humans; He was going to dwell on earth as a human being, as a descendant of David himself.

As a group, read 1 Kings 8:54-61.

What stands out most to you from Solomon's blessing?

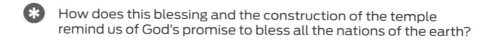 How does this blessing and the construction of the temple remind us of God's promise to bless all the nations of the earth?

The temple was to be a beacon for all nations, not only for Israel. Solomon desired for all nations to hear of the glory of God, and he hoped that all nations would gather and worship the God of Israel. The message of the greatness, mercy, and power of God has always been for all nations. God wanted all those who live apart from Him to call on the name of the Lord.

✚ MISSIONAL Application

Record in this space at least one way you will apply the truth of Scripture as a temple of the Holy Spirit for the glory of God in Jesus Christ.

Personal Study 1

The temple bears God's name.

Read 1 Kings 5:1-5.

Names are powerful. Mention Adolf Hitler, Steve Jobs, Justin Bieber, Barack Obama, Tiger Woods, or Warren Buffet and you're likely to start an interesting conversation in the break room of your office. King Solomon knew the power of names too. He knew the esteem and honor that certain names deserve. This was one of the main reasons he wanted to build a house for the Lord.

Up to this point in redemptive history, Israel's God was not associated with any particular place. He had manifested Himself in visions, in a burning bush, in a pillar of fire, on the mountaintop, in the tabernacle, and with the ark of the covenant. But until now, there was no established place where His people could point and say, "This is the house of our God."

The moment was right because God gave Solomon rest on every side. God did this, not Solomon. God worked and moved to expand the kingdom of Solomon. At this point, unlike in David's time, there was rest and peace all around. God had subdued the enemies of Israel and established them on every side.

The temple was a tangible reminder of what the Lord had done for the nation He loved. He was the One who brought Israel from Egypt. He was the One who gave them His law. He was the One who brought them through the wilderness into a land flowing with milk and honey. He was the sovereign God who saved and established His people. Solomon responded to this sovereign work by erecting a building worthy of the God of heaven.

Another reason—the chief one—Solomon built the temple was because God promised King David that he would (v. 5). Before Solomon was ever born, God declared to David that He would put his son on the throne and establish his kingdom. This promise was now coming to fruition in Solomon's day.

The temple was not only evidence of God's work; it was evidence of God's keeping His word. We serve a God who keeps His promises. God does not play games with His people. He does not string us along only to leave us in the dark. Rather, He is the promise-keeping God who never fails.

In the New Testament, Jesus spoke of Himself as the temple—the embodiment of God. Jesus not only bears God's name, He is God (John 1:1). He accomplished all the work that the Father had given Him to do (John 4:34), and all the promises of God find their yes in Him (2 Cor. 1:20). He came to radically redefine how Israel understood the temple and its place among God's people.

All that God intended to show with the temple, He would show even more so with His own Son, who claimed that He was the true temple (John 2:12-25). For this reason, the name of God is no longer localized to a place—it is found in a Person. We go to Jesus and see the work and promises of God on full display.

What ideas and beliefs do you think were communicated to the Israelites when they visited the temple?

What ideas and beliefs do you think were communicated to people outside Israel when they saw the temple?

What purposes of the temple are fulfilled in Jesus?

Personal Study 2

The temple hosts God's presence.

Read 1 Kings 8:10-14.

After Solomon completed the temple, he gathered all Israel, along with the priests, Levites, and leaders, to bring the ark of the covenant to the Lord's house (vv. 1-9). On that day, God displayed His glory among His people. Just imagine standing among the assembly witnessing this spectacular display of God's glory!

This event further established and confirmed Solomon's kingdom and reign, and it showed yet again God's love and commitment to His people, Israel. Normally, God dwelled in thick darkness (v. 12), in a place where no one could see Him. But now, God had come down to be with His people in the place built for His name and presence. God was so near and real that day that even the priests had to stop what they were doing!

On that day, Israel received the blessing of God Himself. This is the greatest blessing that God can give to His people—Himself. In fact, we see all throughout the Bible that God's intention has always been to dwell among His people. We see this theme from the beginning to the end of Scripture.

- God walked with Adam and Eve in the garden before their sin resulted in banishment from His presence (Gen. 1–3).

- God gave Moses intricate details for the tabernacle and the ark to establish His presence among Israel and meet with them regularly (Ex. 29:42).

- When Israel failed in their faithfulness to God's covenant, the most severe judgment from the Lord was removing Himself from the temple (Ezek. 10:18).

- God's promise to revisit His people and establish them once again was fulfilled in Jesus, who is called "Immanuel," which is translated "God is with us" (Matt. 1:23).

- At the end of history, when all things are set right, we read this promise from Revelation: "God's dwelling is with humanity, and he will live with them. They will be his peoples, and God himself will be with them and will be their God" (Rev. 21:3).

The great hope of the Christian life is not getting things from God; it is getting God Himself. We have a God who wants to be known and who wants us to experience and enjoy His presence.

The New Testament teaches that Jesus is the true temple of God and that as His followers, we also are the temple of God. God dwells in His people through His Holy Spirit. Consider what Peter said about this: "As you come to him, a living stone— rejected by people but chosen and honored by God—you yourselves, as living stones, a spiritual house, are being built to be a holy priesthood to offer spiritual sacrifices acceptable to God through Jesus Christ" (1 Pet. 2:4-5).

Many of us gather for worship and never truly recognize the greatness of the God we are worshiping. Our hearts are filled with distractions, other duties to get to, and anxiety about the week ahead. But if what Peter said is true—and it is—then when we gather with God's people, we are engaging in the most climactic event of our week.

When have you sensed the reality of God's presence? What was it about that time that convinced you it was the Spirit working?

What is your attitude toward gathering for worship with the church? What are some things you can do to prepare for worship to make it more meaningful and edifying?

Personal Study 3

The temple advances God's mission.

Read 1 Kings 8:54-61.

We don't generally associate the nation of Israel with the term *mission*, especially when it comes to the temple. But a phrase that we tend to gloss over in this passage is perhaps the most important thing Solomon prayed here. He blessed the people and offered a prayer for the nation that "all the peoples of the earth know that the LORD is God" (v. 60).

This was one reason God chose the nation of Israel. He did not choose them for their own sake. He chose them for the sake of the nations. He is a global God who desires all the nations to be glad in Him (see Ps. 67). Israel was to be a particular people with a universal purpose—to extend the name and glory of God to the ends of the earth (Ex. 19:5-6).

We see how this plays out in the story of Jonah. God called him to go to the hated and wicked city of Nineveh. Of course, Jonah rebelled and went to Tarshish instead before God sent a great fish to lead Jonah to repentance and back on mission. The book ends with these words from the Lord: "May I not care about the great city of Nineveh, which has more than a hundred and twenty thousand people who cannot distinguish between their right and their left, as well as many animals?" (Jonah 4:11).

This last statement was not only an indictment of Jonah; it was a wake-up call to the nation of Israel. God chose them for the sake of mission—for the sake of blessing the entire world. His choice of Israel did not mean the rejection of other nations but their inclusion through His chosen people (see Rom. 11:11-32)!

The temple in Israel represented what God wanted to do across the whole earth. He wanted to spread His name and fame, not only to Israel but among all the nations so that Habakkuk's words might be fulfilled: "For the earth will be filled with the knowledge of the LORD's glory, as the waters cover the sea" (Hab. 2:14).

The urgency to live on mission is even greater for us as Christians. We are now the temple of God on the earth. God indwells us and fills us as His missional people (see Eph. 2:18-22; 1 Pet. 2:4-5). God called us and chose us for the purpose of representing Him on the earth and spreading His fame to the nations.

As we think of this great task before us, we must understand that it starts with ordinary Christians having ordinary conversations with ordinary people. It starts with you choosing each day to live your life on mission and being available for whatever God wants to do through you. It is virtually impossible to talk about following Jesus without also talking about how to help others follow Him. Following Jesus by necessity means helping others follow Him and obey Him.

As Christians, we are a *saved* people. But we are also a *sent* people. We are sent into the world to bear God's name and make Him known to all people. And one day we will gather around the throne of Jesus Christ and sing, "You are worthy to take the scroll and to open its seals, because you were slaughtered, and you purchased people for God by your blood from every tribe and language and people and nation" (Rev. 5:9).

What should our identity as God's temple, His representatives in the world, communicate to the nations today?

What is your greatest fear when it comes to living on mission for the gospel?

How does God's heart for the world help you overcome these fears?

Solomon's Foolishness Divides the Kingdom

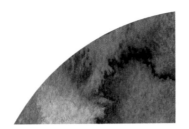
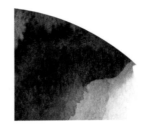
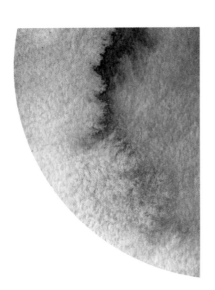

Introducing the Study

God has always desired to live in intimate relationship with His people. We have seen evidence of this in the garden of Eden, through the construction of the tabernacle in the wilderness, and through the building of the temple in Jerusalem. Ultimately, though, this desire of God is most fully expressed through the provision of His Son, Jesus, who is Immanuel—God with us.

 How should God's desire to live in intimacy with you change your perspective of yourself and life?

God used Solomon to build His temple according to His specifications and from the prosperity God had given him. But that same prosperity also led to Solomon straying from the God who had provided it. Despite having been blessed with great wisdom, wealth, and power by God, the king turned from God and showed yet again that no earthly king can be what the people truly need.

What should the Christian's attitude be toward wealth and prosperity?

Setting the Context

When Israel demanded a king like the other nations, God was displeased with their request, not because they wanted a king but because they wanted the *wrong* king and they sought to be like the other nations. God conceded to their desire, but He warned them about **the dangers of kings** whose hearts were not set on following Him.

> How should the presence of God in our lives change our perspective on the world and the desires of our hearts?

Perhaps the saddest example of a wayward king is **King Solomon**. At one time he ruled in wisdom and justice. People from all over the world came to seek an audience with him for his wisdom. His wealth was unmatched, surpassing all the kings of the world in riches. He built the temple of the Lord as a beacon of His glory, and the presence of the Lord filled that structure. Solomon had poised Israel to be a light and blessing to the world. But there was a great and tragic irony to the reign of Solomon.

In spite of Solomon's great wisdom and blessing from the Lord, the king went the other direction and began to stray. Though he was the wisest man in the world, Solomon made **several extremely foolish decisions**. Solomon's life and reign spiraled out of control as he turned from the God who called him and established him as king. As the map on **"The Kingdoms of Israel and Judah"** (p. 83) shows, the judgment and result of Solomon's foolishness was a divided kingdom for his son and descendants after him.

✱ How does the essence of wisdom—the fear of the Lord—figure into our struggle with obedience and disobedience?

✝ CHRIST Connection

Solomon was a king whose reign was marked by prosperity and peace, but in the end, Solomon's sinful compromise led to the division of the kingdom. During His earthly ministry, Jesus spoke of Himself when He claimed "something greater than Solomon is here" (Luke 11:31). Whereas Solomon's sinful choices divided the kingdom, Christ's righteous submission to God established a new unity for God's people.

The Kingdoms of Israel and Judah

PHOENICIA
ARAM
GESHUR
ISRAEL
AMMON
JUDAH
MOAB
EDOM
PHILISTIA
MEDITERRANEAN SEA
DEAD SEA
Negeb
Wilderness
Int

Beirut
Sidon
Ijon
Tyre
Abel beth-maacah
Dan
Mt. Hermon
Damascus
Achzib
Kedesh
Hazor
Lake Huleh
Acco
Chinnereth
Mt. Carmel
Gath-hepher
Sea of Galilee
Aphek
Ashtaroth
Megiddo
Mt. Tabor
Edrei
Dor
Taanach
Jezreel
Mt. Gilboa
Ramoth-gilead
Dothan
Beth-shan
Ibleam
Pehel
Socoh
Jabesh-gilead
Samaria
Tirzah
Mt. Ebal
Shechem
Penuel
Mahanaim
Aphek
Mt. Gerizim
Succoth
Adam
Joppa
Shiloh
Upper Beth-horon
Bethel
Rabbah (Amman)
Lower Beth-horon
Mizpah
Jericho
Gezer
Geba
Heshbon
Aijalon
Ramah
Ashdod
Ekron
Gibeah
Mt. Nebo
Medeba
Gath
Jerusalem
Azekah
Bethlehem
Ashkelon
Mareshah
Beth-zur
Tekoa
Lachish
Adoraim
Hebron
Zihph
Dibon
Gaza
Carmel
Maon
Gerar
Arad
DEAD SEA
Beersheba
Kir-hareseth
Tamar
King's Highway
Bozrah
Kadesh-barnea

- • City
- ★ Capital city
- ○ City (uncertain location)
- ▲ Mountain peak
-   Israel
-   Judah
- —— International roads
- —— Local roads

0 10 20 30 40 50 Miles
0 10 20 30 40 50 Kilometers

32 E
32 N

Continuing the Discussion

 Watch this session's video, and then continue the group discussion using the following guide.

How does Solomon's reign serve as both an example and a warning for us?

In what ways does King Solomon remind us of our need for King Jesus alone?

As a group, read 1 Kings 11:1-8.

Why do you think God specifically warned His people about intermarriage with those from foreign lands?

What does that warning tell you about the nature of marriage and sex?

Solomon knew the warnings, but he foolishly did not listen and married women from other nations. God had warned His people against the practice not because He was against marriage between nations but because He knew that such a marriage would introduce rival gods into the lives of His people and they would lapse into idolatry. And yet, the wisest person to ever live chose to rebel against God, thinking he knew more than Him.

As a group, read 1 Kings 11:9-13.

What was the core reason Solomon experienced the discipline of God? Why is that important to recognize?

Why does God allow us to experience the consequences of our own choices rather than protect us from them all the time?

God is after our hearts. This was His main concern with Solomon; it was not so much that he married foreign women but rather what those marriages did to his heart. As a result of Solomon's sin, the kingdom of Israel would be divided and split from his family. But even in the consequences of sin, God showed Solomon mercy in that this would not happen during his own reign.

As a group, read 1 Kings 12:12-17.

> What can you discern about the character of Rehoboam, the son of Solomon?

> How do these verses further show the consequences of sin?

✱ Why is it important for us to recognize that we are not alone in feeling the effects of our sin—others do as well?

Sin might be private, but its effects always move beyond us. As a result of Solomon's sin, his son and the entire nation were affected. Our good deeds done for the Lord have the potential to bless others with justice, goodness, kindness, and the good news of the gospel. But our sin has the opposite effect—not only does sin bring negative consequences to our own lives, others around us will also feel those effects.

✝ MISSIONAL Application

Record in this space at least one way you will apply the truth of Scripture as one who has been saved from the foolishness of sin.

Personal Study 1

Foolish choices compromise devotion to God.

Read 1 Kings 11:1-8.

Solomon was the greatest king in both wisdom and wealth. God's promise to Abraham looked as if it were coming true: God's people had been rescued; they were living in the land God promised them; they had a good and wise king; and other nations were being blessed by Solomon's wisdom.

If Solomon's story stopped there, we would be applauding him as the greatest king in Israel. We might even wonder if he was at last the long-awaited king whose sons would rule over God's people in God's promised land forever. But unfortunately the story continues. Solomon's compromise and downfall reveal he was not the expected king—another was needed.

Solomon's life is one of the most illustrative pictures of idolatry in the Bible. Idolatry and foolishness go hand in hand. If wisdom means to fear the Lord first and foremost, then foolishness is to place something—anything—above the Lord. Foolish choices *always* accompany idolatry. In Solomon's case, there is no outright rejection of God. He wasn't setting God aside; he was *adding* other gods around the Lord. He wasn't disregarding the Lord altogether; he was *partially* regarding the Lord. He chose to follow Yahweh *alongside* other gods (see Josh. 24:15).

First, it began with a disregard for God's specific instructions. Before God brought Israel to the promised land, He gave them specific commands about how kings were to conduct themselves. They were not to gather much gold and horses for themselves, and they were not to acquire many wives (Deut. 17:14-20). If they did, their hearts would go astray. We see this fleshed out in Solomon's life. He acquired much wealth, vast amounts of horses and chariots, and he had one thousand women in his court. The result? His heart was led astray.

This is how idolatry starts, with a disregard for God's law. In our foolishness we turn away from the Creator and choose instead to worship created things (Rom. 1:18-23). We shun the fountain of true joy and stubbornly build our own dirty wells to drink from (Jer. 2:13).

Idolatry also creates division in our hearts. Something else functions in the place of God. Some other person or experience or pursuit grabs our attention and thoughts. God is slowly pushed away from the center of our lives as our idols demand our attention and affection.

Finally, idolatry leads to destruction. When the apostle Paul talked about the enemies of the cross, he said, "Their end is destruction; their god is their stomach; their glory is in their shame. They are focused on earthly things" (Phil. 3:19). This is the language of idolatry. When something else has our focus and our passion, our end is destruction unless we repent and seek the Lord.

We know that Solomon derailed his kingship and fell under the Lord's judgment through his idolatry. God gave him up to his desires, and Israel suffered as a nation. Idolatry always leaves us fruitless and frustrated and can lead to our downfall.

How do our material possessions affect our spiritual state?

What are some signs that a person has a "divided" heart?

How can you tell if your heart is devoted to the Lord or divided by other pursuits?

Personal Study 2

Foolish choices come with consequences.

Read 1 Kings 11:9-13.

Solomon's father, David, experienced the consequences of sin. When he made the choice to have an adulterous relationship with Bathsheba, their child died as a consequence, and the suffering didn't stop there. Solomon walked a similar path, abandoning his wholehearted commitment to the Lord, and that abandonment brought consequences.

Many times, God will allow our choices to run their course. When we choose to walk foolishly through life, there will always be some manner of consequence. At times, God is willing to give us what our sinful hearts truly desire, so we might see those choices come to destruction. When that happens, we can either remain in our sin or we can repent and acknowledge that true satisfaction is found in Him alone. Consequences, then, can either be a wake-up call or they can be a crushing hammer, depending on how we respond.

When we look at the life of Solomon, we have reason to be both disheartened and encouraged. We are disheartened that he compromised his devotion to God and derailed his kingship. But we should also be encouraged because we know that the story does not end there. Solomon is not our king. He is not the true king. We are only to glance at Solomon and then turn our gaze on the one true King—Jesus.

Despite his great wisdom, wealth, and power, Solomon wasn't the king any of us are looking for. We need a greater king than Solomon. As we come to the New Testament, that is what we find. Let's fast forward to the Gospel of Luke, where Jesus speaks of Himself as greater than Solomon: "The queen of the south will rise up at the judgment with the men of this generation and condemn them, because she came from the ends of the earth to hear the wisdom of Solomon, and look—something greater than Solomon is here" (Luke 11:31).

Solomon in all his greatness wasn't great enough. In the end, he fell woefully short of lasting greatness. But there was something coming after Solomon that was even greater. There is a kind of wisdom that Jesus has that even Solomon needed. Jesus' wisdom not only shows us how to live, His wisdom is what gives us life! Jesus *is* the wisdom we need (see 1 Cor. 1:30).

Jesus, through His life, death, and resurrection, is the wisdom that saves. Ultimate wisdom is found only in Jesus. This is where we must turn if and when we find ourselves in the middle of the consequences of our sin. We can embrace those consequences as God's discipline and return wholeheartedly to the only King who knows how to rule rightly over us with wisdom, love, mercy, and grace.

But we must also be ready to serve others when the wisdom of this world fails them. Proverbs reminds us, "Hope delayed makes the heart sick, but desire fulfilled is a tree of life" (Prov. 13:12). In other words, our joy rises and falls with things we look to for hope and security. If we place our hope in physical fitness and we gain a few pounds or incur an injury, our joy shrinks a bit.

Solomon dazzled the world with his wisdom, riches, and power, yet look at how things ended. He failed. Earthly kings and rulers and powers will always fail us. We must not look to them. We must look to Jesus Christ. He is the same yesterday, today, and forever (Heb. 13:8). He will never leave us or forsake us. His love is constant. His grace is limitless. His mercies are new every day. This is our message to the world.

When have consequences of sin served as a wake-up call for you?

What are some reasons we might avoid talking about Jesus with non-Christians as they struggle with hope or fear? How does Jesus provide precisely what they need in those times?

Personal Study 3

Foolish choices create problems for others.

Read 1 Kings 12:12-17.

Our choices impact those around us, often more than we know. A man who walks in integrity while on a business trip is forging the kind of character that will impact how he relates to his wife, his children, and his friends. They will be impacted in a positive way by his refusal to sin in secret.

On the other hand, when we make foolish choices, we inevitably create problems for those around us. Solomon's son reaped the consequences of his idolatry; so did the nation of Israel, which saw a divided monarchy for the first time in its history. Solomon's sin echoed across the generations.

God told Solomon that his son would have the kingdom torn from his hands and that the kingdom that had enjoyed peace and prosperity during his reign would be divided. Solomon's son, Rehoboam, experienced the fulfillment of God's promises. Though he might have humbled himself and listened to the suffering of his people, the new king instead chose to stand on his own authority, doubling down on the demands his father had for his kingdom.

Rehoboam's pride prevented him from listening to the wise counsel of others. The kingdom was divided, just as God promised it would be. Solomon's idolatry and Rehoboam's pride led Israel into a downward spiral that would eventually result in their exile into Babylon centuries later. This is what happens when we allow foolishness to lead us into idolatry. We may think we are only hurting ourselves, but we are inevitably hurting those around us.

Sadly, Rehoboam had no one to help him come to his senses. In fact, he, like his father, failed to understand that his decisions would have a long-reaching impact on others. He was not living in a vacuum. The reality is that none of us are. Our walk with the Lord is personal, no doubt, but it is not private. We may make decisions in private, but our decisions have public consequences.

In 1 Corinthians 5, the apostle Paul addressed a deviant case of immorality of which the entire church seemed to be proud! Listen to his words to them: "Your boasting is not good. Don't you know that a little leaven leavens the whole batch of dough? Clean out the old leaven so that you may be a new unleavened batch" (1 Cor. 5:6-7). Do you see what Paul was saying? The sin of one individual was *permeating* the entire church. All of them were being impacted by the foolish decisions of one person. Choosing to walk in foolishness will impact those around you.

What is the relationship between foolishness and selfish decisions? Why is selfishness foolish?

How have you been positively impacted by someone else's wise choices?

How have you been negatively impacted by someone else's foolish choices?

Tips for Leading a Small Group

Follow these guidelines to prepare for each group session.

Prayerfully Prepare

Review
Review the weekly material and group questions ahead of time.

Pray
Be intentional about praying for each person in the group. Ask the Holy Spirit to work through you and the group discussion as you point to Jesus each week through God's Word.

Minimize Distractions

Create a comfortable environment. If group members are uncomfortable, they'll be distracted and therefore not engaged in the group experience. Plan ahead by considering these details:

Seating

Temperature

Lighting

Food or Drink

Surrounding Noise

General Cleanliness

At best, thoughtfulness and hospitality show guests and group members they're welcome and valued in whatever environment you choose to gather. At worst, people may never notice your effort, but they're also not distracted. Do everything in your ability to help people focus on what's most important: connecting with God, with the Bible, and with one another.

Include Others

Your goal is to foster a community in which people are welcome just as they are but encouraged to grow spiritually. Always be aware of opportunities to include any people who visit the group and to invite new people to join your group. An inexpensive way to make first-time guests feel welcome or to invite someone to get involved is to give them their own copies of this Bible study book.

Encourage Discussion

A good small-group experience has the following characteristics.

Everyone Participates
Encourage everyone to ask questions, share responses, or read aloud.

No One Dominates—Not Even the Leader
Be sure that your time speaking as a leader takes up less than half of your time together as a group. Politely guide discussion if anyone dominates.

Nobody Is Rushed Through Questions
Don't feel that a moment of silence is a bad thing. People often need time to think about their responses to questions they've just heard or to gain courage to share what God is stirring in their hearts.

Input Is Affirmed and Followed Up
Make sure you point out something true or helpful in a response. Don't just move on. Build community with follow-up questions, asking how other people have experienced similar things or how a truth has shaped their understanding of God and the Scripture you're studying. People are less likely to speak up if they fear that you don't actually want to hear their answers or that you're looking for only a certain answer.

God and His Word Are Central
Opinions and experiences can be helpful, but God has given us the truth. Trust God's Word to be the authority and God's Spirit to work in people's lives. You can't change anyone, but God can. Continually point people to the Word and to active steps of faith.

How to Use the Leader Guide

Prepare to Lead

Each session of the Leader Guide is designed to be **torn out** so you, the leader, can have this front-and-back page with you as you lead your group through the session.

Watch the session teaching video and **read through the session content** with the Leader Guide tear-out in hand and notice how it supplements each section of the study.

Use the **Session Objective** in the Leader Guide to help focus your preparation and leadership in the group session.

Questions and Answers

✴ Questions in the session content with **this icon** have some sample answers provided in the Leader Guide, if needed, to help you jump-start the conversation or steer the conversation.

Setting the Context

This section of the session always has an **infographic** on the opposite page. The Leader Guide provides an activity to help your group members interact with the content communicated through the infographic.

MISSIONAL Application

The Leader Guide provides a **MISSIONAL Application statement** about how Christians should respond to the truth of God's Word. Read this statement to the group and then direct them to record in the blank space provided in their book at least one way they will respond on a personal level, remembering that all of Scripture points to the gospel of Jesus Christ.

Pray

Conclude each group session with a prayer. **A brief sample prayer** is provided at the end of each Leader Guide tear-out.

Session 1 · Leader Guide

Session Objective

Show how God's people continued to rebel against Him and demanded a king who, just as God warned, failed them. Saul looked the part, but he revealed that our hope cannot be placed on any person—our hope must rest in Christ alone.

Introducing the Study

Use these answers as needed for the question highlighted in this section.

- So He can bless them as His special people.
- To preserve them from the sinfulness, death, and destruction associated with the ways of the world.
- So they will be a light to the nations about how to live with the one true God.

Setting the Context

Use these answers as needed for the question highlighted in this section.

- We should reject the patterns of this sinful world and the sins that go with it.
- We should strive to follow and obey everything Jesus commanded.
- We should tell others about Jesus' goodness and grace so they too will bow to Him as their King.

Use the following activity to help group members see how Samuel connects to previous Old Testament figures and points forward to Jesus Christ.

Encourage group members to review **"Samuel's Life"** (p. 11), and ask the following questions: "What are some ways Samuel connects to the Bible stories we have studied thus far in the storyline of Scripture?" "How does Samuel's life point forward to Jesus?" Then explain some of these connections as follows:

- Samuel was miraculously born to a barren woman, much like Isaac, Jacob, and Esau. *All of these miraculous births point forward to the virgin birth of Jesus.*

- Samuel was given to the Lord, and he served in the tabernacle under Eli, so he functioned like a priest. *Jesus is our great high priest and our sacrifice.*

- Samuel proclaimed the word of the Lord and led the people like Moses and Joshua. *Jesus is the very Word of God who became flesh and leads His people.*

- Samuel was a judge like Deborah, Gideon, and Samson and brought peace while he was alive. *Jesus is the judge of the living and the dead, and His peace is eternal.*

Continuing the Discussion

Watch this session's video, and then as part of the group discussion, use these answers as needed for the questions highlighted in this section.

1 Samuel 8:4-9,19-20

- Making plans on our own without any thought to God's will or His mission for us.
- When we choose to sin, we are essentially rejecting God's rule over our lives.
- Refusing to stand up for what is good and right when the world rejects God's ways.

1 Samuel 13:6-9,13-14

- God desires humility and patience in His people.
- God is concerned with our obedience.
- God wants His people to have a heart that follows after His.

1 Samuel 15:10-11,22-23

- We should desire to read and study the Word of God.
- We should desire to obey the Word of God and put His teachings into practice.
- We should proclaim God's Word as truth and grace to a world that is far from Him.

Share the following statement with the group. Then direct them to record in the space provided in their book at least one way they will apply the truth of Scripture as a humble servant of the King of kings.

✝ MISSIONAL Application

Because we have trusted in Christ, the King of kings, for our salvation, we seek to put away all disobedience and submit fully to Him so that the world will experience redemption through Him and enter into God's kingdom.

Close your group in prayer, thanking God that He does for us what we cannot do for ourselves—change our own hearts.

Session 2 · Leader Guide

Session Objective

Show the contrast between Saul, who looked like a king but failed, and David, who didn't look like a king but trusted in God and delivered God's people.

Introducing the Study

Use these answers as needed for the question highlighted in this section.

- Even when we stumble in our faith and sin, God knows our hearts.
- While my works may look good, God examines our works and our motives.
- We don't have to live up to other people's external standards; we aim to be people who follow after the heart of God.

Setting the Context

Use these answers as needed for the question highlighted in this section.

- Our primary read of others cannot be their outward appearance.
- We should view every professing Christian as a work in progress because God sees the heart and changes the hearts of His people.
- No matter one's outward appearance and actions, no one is beyond God's sight and God's reach to save.

Use the following activity to help group members see how Saul and David contrast with and foreshadow Jesus, the King of kings.

Ask group members to look over **"The King of Kings"** (p. 23) and to point out some ways Saul contrasts with David *(different tribe; Saul's description is physical, but David's is spiritual; Saul tried to kill David, but David spared Saul's life)*. Then ask group members to point out some ways David foreshadows Jesus, the King of kings *(David is Jesus' ancestor; while David was a man after God's own heart, he still sinned, but Jesus never sinned; David wanted to build a temple for God, but Jesus is the true temple of God; David spared Saul, and Jesus prayed for forgiveness for those who crucified Him)*.

Read this paragraph to transition to the next part of the study.

Saul's reign over Israel included a few bright spots but was overshadowed by his evil acts. David, on the other hand, was a man after God's own heart, yet he too succumbed to temptation and sin with disastrous consequences. While David would become the benchmark of obedience for every other king that followed him, only Jesus measures up and surpasses him as the King of kings and Lord of lords.

Continuing the Discussion

Watch this session's video, and then as part of the group discussion, use these answers as needed for the questions highlighted in this section.

1 Samuel 16:1,6-13

- David was the youngest and smallest in his family.
- His role in the household was that of tending sheep, being out in the fields alone all day.
- His own father didn't invite him to the sacrifice and ceremony with Samuel.

1 Samuel 17:23-26,34-37

- David was concerned not for himself, his brothers, the army, or the king but for the glory of God.
- David boldly proclaimed his faith in God before King Saul, saying that God would hand Goliath over to him.
- David recounted stories from his past about how God had delivered him from lions and bears as he protected his sheep.

1 Samuel 17:45-51

- David's victory seemed to come in spite of certain death.
- The enemy of God's people fell in judgment before the anointed king; in an even greater way, the enemies of God's people have fallen in judgment before the anointed King who died and rose again.
- Both David and Jesus fought for the glory of God and the salvation of God's people.

Share the following statement with the group. Then direct them to record in the space provided in their book at least one way they will apply the truth of Scripture as a herald of the good news that Jesus has defeated the enemies of sin and death.

 MISSIONAL Application

Because we have been forgiven through the power of the cross, we don't pursue the nations in judgment but with the message of grace so that all may hear the good news and be swept up into the glorious love and grace of God.

Close your group in prayer, praising God that He fought the battle that we could not and gave us the victory we did not earn.

Session 3 · Leader Guide

Session Objective

Show how God's plan was for His people to be ruled by Jesus, the perfect King who would establish an eternal kingdom.

Introducing the Study

Use these answers as needed for the question highlighted in this section.

- We don't want to idolize the man David because he too falls short of the glory of God.
- David serves a role in God's plan of redemption, but it cannot overshadow God's purpose in David's life—to one day reveal Jesus, the Son of God.
- No human being can lead and represent God's people as he should; only Jesus fulfills God's expectations for the king.

Setting the Context

Use these answers as needed for the question highlighted in this section.

- We will be disappointed by the shortcomings of an earthly ruler.
- An earthly ruler is prone to take our hopes and use them for his or her own selfish desires.
- We can ruin our witness for the true King if we allow ourselves to put our hopes in an earthly ruler, who will surely fail.

Use the following activity to help group members see the significance of a Christ-centered reading of Scripture.

Ask group members what they know about David and Solomon as kings and people. *(David defeated Goliath; David spared Saul's life; David trusted in God; David wrote psalms; Solomon was the wisest person ever to live; Solomon wrote many proverbs.)* Emphasizing the praiseworthy aspects of David and Solomon, refer your group members to **"Seeing Jesus in the Kings"** (p. 35), and ask them to call out ways Jesus surpasses both David and Solomon, both from the infographic and other ways they may know from Scripture. Then ask the following question: "What is significant about Jesus being greater than these two towering figures from the Old Testament?"

Continuing the Discussion

Watch this session's video, and then as part of the group discussion, use these answers as needed for the questions highlighted in this section.

2 Samuel 7:8-11a

- Jesus is the One who defeats our enemies of sin and death through His death and resurrection.
- Our battles in life are ultimately not against flesh and blood but against our spiritual enemies, and only Jesus can defeat them.
- All of the work needed for our salvation from sin is accomplished by Jesus; we rest from our work in Him.

2 Samuel 7:11b-17

- God would raise up a descendant from David whose kingdom would be established forever.
- The Son of David is the One who builds the perfect and eternal house for God's name.
- Only the throne of Jesus endures before God forever.

2 Samuel 7:18-29

- God's sovereignty and omniscience.
- The greatness and uniqueness of God.
- The grace and love of God.
- God's goodness, faithfulness, and glory.

Share the following statement with the group. Then direct them to record in the space provided in their book at least one way they will apply the truth of Scripture as a recipient of God's grace and rest through faith in Jesus Christ, God's forever King.

✚ MISSIONAL Application

Because we have experienced the mercy and grace of our King, we offer ourselves fully to His service so that we might reveal Jesus Christ to the world so that others would find everlasting rest in His kingdom.

Close your group in prayer, praising God that His promises to us are based on Jesus, not our own work or goodness.

Session 4 · Leader Guide

Session Objective

Show that David was a great but imperfect king who desperately needed God's grace just as we all do, and through His repentance, God lavished it upon him.

Introducing the Study

Use these answers as needed for the question highlighted in this section.

- Being a coheir of God with Christ means that all the treasures of heaven are ours, supremely that of God's presence and favor.
- Eternal life is secure in Jesus for those who repent of their sin and turn to Him in faith for salvation.
- Security here on earth is always a fragile notion, subject to the whims of human beings in authority or those who defy authority, but no one can snatch God's people from Jesus' hand.

Setting the Context

Use these answers as needed for the question highlighted in this section.

- Christians strive to love and pray for their enemies rather than seek vengeance.
- The world lives for pride and self-promotion, but Christians should have the attitude of Christ, one of humility and self-sacrifice for the benefit of others.
- Accumulating wealth and stuff is a passion of the world, but Christians should be generous and sacrificial for the sake of the gospel mission.

Use the following activity to help group members see how our attitude toward the blessings of God determines whether or not we live for His glory or fall into sin.

Call attention to **"David's Enemies"** (p. 47). Ask group members the following questions: "Why should David's actions with regard to King Saul be included as a victory over his enemies?" "Do you think victories embolden or weaken faith? Why?" "Why should we all view ourselves as a potential enemy to our obedience in the faith?"

Read this paragraph to transition to the next part of the study.

Victories from the Lord in David's life emboldened his faith. Recall that the Lord handed lions and bears over to David as he defended his sheep, and this gave him confidence to face Goliath for the glory of the Lord. But his successive military victories gave him the idea that he could relax at home, which led to his sin. The result of victories in our lives depends upon our attitude and the focus of our lives.

Continuing the Discussion

Watch this session's video, and then as part of the group discussion, use these answers as needed for the questions highlighted in this section.

2 Samuel 11:1-5

- We should resist going to places where we know we will be tempted.
- We should keep people around us who help to hold us accountable in our actions.
- We should be faithful to fulfill our duties and responsibilities.

2 Samuel 11:6-17

- In Jesus' crucifixion, we can see that truly the wages of sin is death.
- Because the Father sent His Son to save people from their sin, we can know that forgiveness is available when we repent and turn again to Jesus in faith.
- The Holy Spirit convicts us of our sin so we can repent of it.

Psalm 51:4-10

- David is humble instead of prideful.
- David is broken over his sin instead of trying to cover it up.
- David desires purity before God rather than the appearance of goodness before human beings.

Share the following statement with the group. Then direct them to record in the space provided in their book at least one way they will apply the truth of Scripture as a repentant and forgiven sinner through faith in Jesus Christ.

MISSIONAL Application

Because we are a forgiven people, we live with joy and appropriate transparency before others so that they too might repent and find forgiveness of their sin in Jesus Christ.

Close your group in prayer, thanking God that we cannot out-sin His grace and asking Him for courage to admit our own weakness.

Session 5 · Leader Guide

Session Objective

Show that Solomon asked for and was given wisdom by God, but looking ahead, even that would not be enough to make him the king the people needed.

Introducing the Study

Use these answers as needed for the question highlighted in this section.

- A broken and humbled heart.
- A desire not to do the same sin again.
- A renewed desire to obey and glorify God for His grace in Jesus.

Setting the Context

Use these answers as needed for the question highlighted in this section.

- We are sinful people prone to go our own way instead of God's.
- We have been so blessed by God that we forget that He gives us all we need.
- The natural way of the world is to earn your own keep, and we carry that mind-set over to our spiritual lives.

Use the following activity to help group members see that the wisdom of Solomon has been given to us in Scripture and points us to Jesus.

Ask group members to look at **"Solomon's Wisdom"** (p. 59), and explain that wisdom literature in Scripture is meant to teach people how to live rightly and faithfully in the world that God has made, even though it has been tainted by sin. Also note that the Bible books listed are attributed to Solomon, the wisest man ever to live. Call on some volunteers to pick a verse or two out of the Book of Proverbs to read for the group. Then ask the following questions: "What are your thoughts about the fact that Solomon's wisdom was inspired by God and recorded in Scripture for our benefit?" "How would you explain 'the fear of the LORD' in your own words?" "Why should we remember that all wisdom is meant to point us to Jesus?"

Read this paragraph to transition to the next part of the study.

For all his wisdom, Solomon would make some huge mistakes in his life, demonstrating the need for a greater wisdom—Jesus Christ. But Solomon became wise in the first place because he recognized he needed wisdom and that true wisdom came from the God willing to give it to those who ask for it.

Continuing the Discussion

Watch this session's video, and then as part of the group discussion, use these answers as needed for the questions highlighted in this section.

1 Kings 3:5-9

- God created the world and everything in it.
- Only God's will is perfect and good, so true wisdom can only come from Him.
- All other sources of wisdom come from people tainted by sin, people who operate from a desire to please and elevate themselves.

1 Kings 3:10-15

- Solomon was humble in his thoughts about himself.
- Solomon turned to God as the only One who could help him.
- Solomon's willing heart meant God could display His glory in him.

1 Kings 3:16-28

- Wisdom that does not lead to justice is self-centered and from the world, not from God.
- Wisdom rejects favoritism and hypocrisy, which is key to justice in the world.
- Wisdom leading to justice displays for all the world to see that God is truly the Creator and Sustainer of everything and everyone who exists.

Share the following statement with the group. Then direct them to record in the space provided in their book at least one way they will apply the truth of Scripture as a recipient of the wisdom of God in Jesus Christ.

✝ MISSIONAL Application

Because we have received God's perfect wisdom in Christ Jesus, we depend on His wisdom from above to live as a testimony to our all-wise God.

Close your group in prayer, asking God to give you and your group wisdom to make decisions in everyday life that bring Him glory and lead to justice in the world.

Session 6 · Leader Guide

Session Objective

Show how through the temple, God provided a new and better way to be with His people than the tabernacle that had preceded it. The temple would be a place where God's name was lifted high in worship and where His people could draw near to Him and show the nations around them the Lord is God.

Introducing the Study

Use these answers as needed for the question highlighted in this section.

- The temple was a place for the presence of God to dwell, which is now accomplished for us in Jesus and through the Holy Spirit.
- The temple was where sacrifices for sin were made, and Jesus is the sacrifice that opens the door for our relationship with God the Father.
- The temple was a place of holy reverence for the name of God; Jesus obeyed the Father completely for the glory of His name in the world.

Setting the Context

Use these answers as needed for the question highlighted in this section.

- God is the same yesterday, today, and forever, so God's expectations in the temple still have some application for us today.
- The temple foreshadows the coming of Jesus.
- The temple helps Christians understand the purpose of the church, the community of believers in Jesus Christ.

Use the following activity to help group members see that the temple communicated the holiness of God and pointed forward to the true temple in Jesus.

Call attention to the illustration of **"The Temple"** (p. 71). Ask group members to call out what they see in the picture *(walls, an altar, a basin of water, pillars, steps, a door)*. Then ask the group to consider what these things are meant to communicate about God and access to Him.

Read this paragraph to transition to the next part of the study.

In the temple, the path to relationship with God is barred by walls and doors. Only priests can enter into His holy presence, and that only by way of sacrifice. The temple screams out the holiness of God and His expectations from His people. But access to God the Father now comes to us freely by faith in Jesus Christ, the true temple of God.

Continuing the Discussion

Watch this session's video, and then as part of the group discussion, use these answers as needed for the questions highlighted in this section.

1 Kings 5:1-5

- The temple was a magnificent structure designed and built by the wisest person in the world, who had received his wisdom for the work from God.
- It showed that the blessings experienced by the nation of Israel were attributed by the people to the one true God.
- It would demonstrate the glory and the holiness of God for the whole world to see.

1 Kings 8:10-14

- With humility and awe for God's glory.
- With praise and adoration for God.
- With blessing communicated to others for what the Lord has done.

1 Kings 8:54-61

- The temple would be a place where all the peoples on earth could seek out the presence of God, even though He is not constrained to a particular place.
- The people of God were to live in holiness and obedience because of God's presence in their midst, which would lead to justice in their nation and be a light to the world.
- This temple alone of all the temples to gods in the world was inhabited visibly and tangibly by the one true God with the display of His glory.

Share the following statement with the group. Then direct them to record in the space provided in their book at least one way they will apply the truth of Scripture as a temple of the Holy Spirit for the glory of God in Jesus Christ.

✚ MISSIONAL Application

Because the presence of God indwells us, we are to obey Him and make Him known so that the original purpose of the temple can be fulfilled—that the people of the earth will know our God is King.

Close your group in prayer, praying that you and your group would have a growing desire to see the name of Jesus lifted high among all the nations of the earth.

Session 7 · Leader Guide

Session Objective

Show how as great as it was, Solomon's wisdom failed to protect him from sin, and in the end, just like Saul and David, Solomon failed to be the king God's people need.

Introducing the Study

Use these answers as needed for the question highlighted in this section.

- • I should view myself as worthwhile and valuable.
- • I should strive to see myself as God sees me, not as the world sees me or even according my own sinful perceptions of myself.
- • My life should reflect the holiness and love of the holy God who loves me.

Setting the Context

Use these answers as needed for the question highlighted in this section.

- • If we fear the Lord, we will obey Him in love and respect.
- • Disobedience shows that we do not fear the Lord in some aspect of our lives.
- • In order to obey God from the heart, we must believe He exists and rewards those who seek Him, so the fear of the Lord involves faith in who God is and what He has said.

Use the following activity to help group members see the spiritual fallout of foolishness and sin.

Point your group members to the map on **"The Kingdoms of Israel and Judah"** (p. 83). Explain that the throne for David's descendants continued in the Southern Kingdom of Judah. Then ask the following questions:

- What problems would you expect to see from a once united people now divided into two? *(conflict, competition, war, distrust, death and destruction)*

- How does a divided kingdom impact God's promises to Abraham, Isaac, Jacob, and David? *(God promised to bless all the people on earth through Abraham's descendants, but how can they bless others when they can't live together in peace? David's throne was to be established forever; Jacob's descendants are struggling in opposition to God and failing to live up to His holiness.)*

- What would you expect the promised King to accomplish as a part of His rule in the name of God? *(to unify the peoples of God; to bring peace and order; to rule completely in wisdom and with justice)*

Continuing the Discussion

Watch this session's video, and then as part of the group discussion, use these answers as needed for the questions highlighted in this section.

1 Kings 11:1-8

- Marriage and sex are conduits for intimacy between a husband and wife, which includes the sharing of minds and hearts, whether for good or for ill.
- Marriage and sex should not be taken lightly as a husband and wife become one.
- Being intimately involved with another person is more than just a physical act; it has spiritual ramifications as well.

1 Kings 11:9-13

- Solomon's heart had turned away from the Lord.
- All sin comes from shifting loyalties in our hearts: either we are turned toward the Lord in love and loyalty or we are turned away from Him in sin.
- God's commands are not about distancing the nations but preserving the holiness of His people so the nations will see in them the Lord's goodness.

1 Kings 12:12-17

- Considering the consequences of our sin for both ourselves and others can help us choose to act wisely and faithfully.
- What we do, whether good or evil, has an impact on our gospel mission.
- Recognizing the fallout of sin should lead us to accountability for ourselves and the conviction to care about the sin in the lives of others.

Share the following statement with the group. Then direct them to record in the space provided in their book at least one way they will apply the truth of Scripture as one who has been saved from the foolishness of sin.

✝ MISSIONAL Application

Because we have been forgiven of all our sin through Christ, we proclaim the foolishness of relying on our own wisdom for salvation and lift up Jesus as the only hope for the world.

Close your group in prayer, asking God to help you proactively guard your hearts against temptation that will make you stray from Him.

THE SACRIFICE PLEASING TO GOD

is a broken spirit.
You will not despise a broken
and humbled heart, God.

PSALM 51:17

FROM COVER
TO COVER,

the Bible is the story of God's plan to redeem sinners through Jesus—the gospel. Gospel Foundations tells that story.

Be sure to take advantage of the following resources if you're planning a churchwide study. Even the *Single Group Starter Pack* offers significant savings.

CHURCH LAUNCH KIT (DIGITAL)

Want to take your entire church through Gospel Foundations? You'll want a *Church Launch Kit*. It includes sermon outlines, promotional graphics, and a Wordsearch Bible digital library for all leaders valued at $330. The *Kit* comes complimentary with every *Church Starter Pack*. Also available separately.

$29.99

Order online, call 800.458.2772, or visit the LifeWay Christian Store serving you.

STARTER PACKS

You can save money and time by purchasing starter packs for your group or church. Every *Church Starter Pack* includes a digital *Church Launch Kit* and access to a digital version of the *Leader Kit* videos.

Single Group Starter Pack
(10 *Bible Study Books*, 1 *Leader Kit*)
$99.99

Church Starter Pack - Small
(50 *Bible Study Books*, 5 *Leader Kit* DVDs, *Church Launch Kit*)
$449.99

Church Starter Pack - Medium
(100 *Bible Study Books*, 10 *Leader Kit* DVDs, *Church Launch Kit*)
$799.99

Church Starter Pack - Large
(500 *Bible Study Books*, 50 *Leader Kit* DVDs, *Church Launch Kit*)
$3495.99

LifeWay.com/GospelFoundations

Prices and availability subject to change without notice.

GOSPEL FOUNDATIONS

The Coming Rescue

| VOL. 4 | 2 KINGS — MALACHI |

A Year Through the Storyline of Scripture   LifeWay

Continue your study of the bigger story of Scripture.

———

The Coming Rescue illustrates that even though God's people have failed to love and obey Him repeatedly, God continues to pursue them, extend His faithful love to them, and advance His plan to redeem them from sin through Jesus. In this volume, God's people are enslaved once again, having forsaken the true God for idols made by human hands. But even though they run from Him, God continues to pursue them. Learn how God pursued His people with a promise—the rescue from their captivity to sin, and the coming of their Redeemer. (7 sessions)

Bible Study Book $9.99
Leader Kit $29.99

Group Directory

Name: _____   Name: _____

Home Phone: _____   Home Phone: _____

Mobile Phone: _____   Mobile Phone: _____

Email: _____   Email: _____

Social Media: _____   Social Media: _____

Name: _____   Name: _____

Home Phone: _____   Home Phone: _____

Mobile Phone: _____   Mobile Phone: _____

Email: _____   Email: _____

Social Media: _____   Social Media: _____

Name: _____   Name: _____

Home Phone: _____   Home Phone: _____

Mobile Phone: _____   Mobile Phone: _____

Email: _____   Email: _____

Social Media: _____   Social Media: _____

Name: _____   Name: _____

Home Phone: _____   Home Phone: _____

Mobile Phone: _____   Mobile Phone: _____

Email: _____   Email: _____

Social Media: _____   Social Media: _____

Name: _____   Name: _____

Home Phone: _____   Home Phone: _____

Mobile Phone: _____   Mobile Phone: _____

Email: _____   Email: _____

Social Media: _____   Social Media: _____

Name: _____   Name: _____

Home Phone: _____   Home Phone: _____

Mobile Phone: _____   Mobile Phone: _____

Email: _____   Email: _____

Social Media: _____   Social Media: _____